D1576525

TROUT FISHING
IN THE UK
AND IRELAND

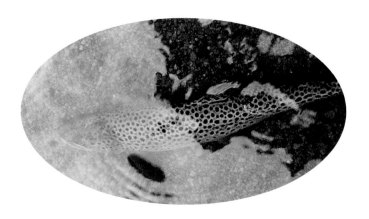

TROUT FISHING IN THE UK AND IRELAND

TECHNIQUES AND TACTICS

LESLEY CRAWFORD

SWAN·HILL
PRESS

Copyright © 2006 Lesley Crawford

First published in the UK in 2006
by Swan Hill Press, an imprint of Quiller Publishing Ltd

British Library Cataloguing-in-Publication Data
A catalogue record for this book
is available from the British Library

ISBN 1 904057 58 6
     978 1 904057 58 1

The right of Lesley Crawford to be identified as the author of this work has
been asserted in accordance with the Copyright, Design and Patent Act 1988

All photography by Lesley Crawford unless otherwise stated

Title page photo by P. Trotter

The information in this book is true and complete to the best of our knowledge.
All recommendations are made without any guarantee on the part of the Publisher,
who also disclaims any liability incurred in connection with the use of this data or
specific details.

All rights reserved. No part of this book may be reproduced or transmitted in
any form or by any means, electronic or mechanical including photocopying,
recording or by any information storage and retrieval system, without permission
from the Publisher in writing.

Printed in China

Swan Hill Press
An imprint of Quiller Publishing Ltd
Wykey House, Wykey, Shrewsbury, SY4 1JA
Tel: 01939 261616 Fax: 01939 261606
E-mail: info@quillerbooks.com
Website: www.countrybooksdirect.com

'Many go fishing all their lives without knowing that it is not fish they are after'

H D Thoreau

ACKNOWLEDGEMENTS

Thanks to all those fellow anglers and friends who have given so freely of their time and expertise. Amongst them are Colin Chartres, Ron Crawford, Joe Gallagher, Mike Gleave, George Helling, Andrew Johnston, Alan Kirkpatrick, Ruth Mettler, Stevie Munn, Pat O'Reilly, Nica and David Prichard, Richard Slocock, John Todd, Patrick Trotter, Andy Walker, David Wood of Tourism Ireland.

Contents

SECTION 2

ENGLAND

WALES

SECTION 5

River Maine Northern Ireland

INTRODUCTION

The British Isles are but a little dot on the world's fishing map; they would fit in a corner of some of the larger American States and would disappear without trace into Africa. Even today a passing tourist might be somewhat surprised to learn that despite our size, we actually have four separate countries England, Ireland, Scotland and Wales contained within our tiny boundaries. Each of these countries has strikingly different languages and cultures and all have practised trout fishing whether for food or for sport from at least the twelfth century if not earlier. Given the very diverse customs and traditions at work it is hardly surprising that different fishing skills have evolved in our treasured sport. When discussing British trout angling, visitors are not always aware there is a deal of difference between say stalking trout on a Welsh river and fishing Scottish loch style, casting a delicate line over an English chalk stream or taking a drift on a vast Irish lough.

For such a small area the British Isles has a huge and complex variety of trout angling skills in play. This book sets out to highlight the differences in fishing techniques across the UK and Ireland, looking at how these came about and where they are heading in the twenty-first century. From the rugged north of Scotland to the deepest shires of southern England along with Welsh valleys and the green lands of Ireland, this book is essentially an account of UK and Irish fishing crafts and customs lovingly developed by generations of anglers on their home waters. Distinctions are made between specialist angling practices and a few very special cornerstones of trout fishing from across the country are described to help bring to life the various local nuances. Be assured any water selected as a pertinent example shows a uniquely British flavour, these are places where founding techniques where first developed and more often than not, these skills will have gone on to become standard practice across the land if not further afield.

For most trout anglers whether visiting a new water or enjoying a local one, the intrinsic joy of their fishing should lie in using methods appropriate for that unique area. In doing so they will shadow the learning curve of many national pioneering anglers who have gone before them and the experience should be a long and pleasurable one. The various inherent angling skills of Scotland, England, Ireland and Wales have therefore been carefully researched with a view to helping you better enjoy inspiring and educational fishing. You will learn why some of the locally devised angling techniques are still fully employed, why some have fallen by the wayside and why new adaptations have sometimes been absorbed across national borders. Fishing any new water can sometimes be daunting; this book should make you better informed before you begin and make your day that much more agreeable.

While this book provides a thorough insight into the different styles of trout angling across the land, comparing them and highlighting essential differences, it is not an across the board guide book as such. There are already plenty of these snapshot tomes which really amount to long lists of venues. Instead this book invokes essential history giving angling methods a sense of place by showing how different fishing techniques evolved. It relates the old to the new and hopefully will encourage all trout anglers to try different experiences while appreciating more of what has been on their doorstep for a very long time.

I've much enjoyed compiling this work, it's been a tremendous pleasure to meet like minded spirits in diverse situations to exchange views and look at trout fishing from some wonderfully different perspectives. Geographically we are small but our trout angling heritage is huge as are our fishing opportunities. Come and join me now on this quest to learn more of the trout fishing techniques of the UK and Ireland...

SECTION 1

SCOTLAND

Chapter 1

THE TROUT OF SCOTLAND

In the Beginning…

It goes without saying the unsullied lochs and sparkling rivers of this country have teemed with trout since the first fish colonised the country after the last Ice Age. Right from earliest times Scotland's crystal waters have held both brown and sea trout in abundance alongside excellent salmon populations. Given their abundance, both trout and salmon were held in great esteem by the Scots providing them with a rich food resource, indeed fish formed an important and easily obtained part of the rural diet. It is quite extraordinary to reflect on the fact that at one time there was so profuse a supply of game fish notably salmon, that it became an unwritten rule that, in some parts of Scotland, farm workers were not to be fed wild salmon more than five days in a week!

With game fish so prolific it is worth looking in particular at the evolution of the trout of Scotland as it is a particularly interesting one. Firstly there exists a relatively ignored, but nevertheless important ancient division between the characteristics of the trout of the west coast of Scotland when compared with their brethren inhabiting the east. Many thousands of years ago, the western seaboard trout were territorial beasts, relatively solitary by nature and more bronzed in hue, much akin to the ferox we know today. The silver liveried trout of the eastern seaboard on the other hand were more adventurous creatures given to an altogether more roving pelagic lifestyle, one which equates more to the sea trout and to a certain extent the modern Loch Leven trout. Over some years the migrating trout of the east coast explored Scottish coastlines and eventually they made their way round the north coast of Scotland to team up with the resident trout in the rivers of the west coast. This intermingling of strains produced hybrid fish, still marvellous in quality but a little more mixed in genetic nature. Of course all this took place aeons of years ago nevertheless it shows how the wild trout populations of Scotland came about and that even today it is not always purely accidental when you come across trout exhibiting different behavioural characteristics in different parts of the country.

While the old Gaelic name for the trout was 'breac' which meant speckled one as in 'Lochan nam Breac' (loch of speckled trout) or 'breac buidhe' (golden trout) the designation did not continue in the vernacular except in loch place names. Even then the deliberate anglicising of the Gaelic language meant that breac was often spelt incorrectly or missed out. The English name of 'trout' seems to have predominated from the early eighteenth century onward coinciding with various historical cross border spats between the Scots and English during which apparently rebellious Scots and their language were quelled and quashed. During the nineteenth century in keeping with English demands to further scientific knowledge and discover 'new' trout populations, Scotland also saw its native trout split into separate classes. The fish were categorised into distinct groups with names such as Leven trout, Croispol trout and Orkney sea trout (why sea trout were only recognised in Orkney is unknown for they were prolific in virtually all Scottish rivers and many lochs at this time) along with some more obscure names like grey trout, golden trout, humped back trout and parr marked trout, these groupings being mainly found in the highlands of Scotland. In addition there was at one time a flourishing population of trout in the Assynt area of Sutherland which were virtually identical in character to the Irish gillaroo. It has never been conclusively proven that these trout were native Scottish fish or were in fact introduced from Ireland where the main gillaroo population occurs in Lough Melvin.

The 'Scottish' classes of trout were recorded at a similar time to the English sourced Gunther categorisations of *Salmo fario* (river trout) and *Salmo ferox* (lake trout). Scientists of that era initially had identified these 'new' trout populations as different isolated species each with their own genetic make up. It was only in the latter half of the twentieth century that the separate species idea was dropped from Scottish trout and all trout were lumped into the one class, *Salmo trutta*. Interestingly this concept is itself under review again following research carried out in Ireland by Professor Ferguson of Queen's University Belfast (see page 149). Suffice to say that whatever the names and species make up, there are still wonderfully diverse and distinct trout populations remaining in Scotland to this day. These fish have different characteristics and colouration and are much admired by those who angle for them. Whatever their creed, Scotland's trout are a sport fish par excellence.

Stocking – Introductions and Interventions

During the 1800s two major events happened to change the quiet unsullied life of Scotland's indigenous trout forever. Firstly industrialisation meant pollution on a considerable scale particularly in the rivers of Scotland's southern central belt near the cities of Glasgow and Edinburgh. This led to a loss of local trout habitat and an unfortunate depletion of stocks in watercourses near the main centres of human population. In the drive toward industrialisation, scant regard was paid to the well being of freshwater fish with rivers being used as little more than open drains for sewage and/or industrial effluent. As the years went by, the trout populations near the heavily peopled lowland southerly quarters of Scotland began to decline in number in stark contrast to the trout of remoter parts of the north highlands which remained relatively unscathed. Effectively this split the country's trout populations more or less into two halves, one thriving and one slowly declining in nature.

At the same time as the Industrial Revolution was starting its environmental downturn the popularity of trout fishing rose sharply. Increased wealth amongst the late nineteenth century merchants and industrialists meant more leisure time and fishing was seen as the ideal recreation. It is more than a little ironic that those who were indirectly helping to pollute southern Scotland's watercourses were at the same time demanding more fish in them! In those days success in trout fishing was judged by the numbers of fish caught and to meet anglers' growing expectations of catching lots of trout at one go, the adding of new stock into Scotland's freshwaters began in earnest. In line with English stocking doctrine of the 1800s any inland water larger than a hectare was deemed suitable for introducing trout and many waters saw trout added to them whether it was necessary or not. Initially brown trout reared in Scottish and some Northern England hatcheries were the first choice; rainbows were only occasionally used at first as it was generally thought they escaped too quickly down any outflow, hardly surprising given their inherent migratory tendencies. While in some cases native brood stock was used to rear local trout in hatcheries near to the blossoming fisheries, there was also a fair amount of transportation of fish around the length and breadth of the country. It must be remembered however that while brown trout were happily reared and introduced for sport in inland waters, it does not appear that sea trout as a migratory fish were commercially farmed on such a national scale. This may relate to the fact that river anglers demanded salmon first and more attention was paid to rearing salmon than migratory trout which were often seen as little more than pests in the big fish rivers.

With all this new 'stockie' blood being introduced it was goodbye to many inherent pure-blooded Scottish native trout and hello to an interbred race, still of superb quality but of a more mixed origin. The practice of stock additions was done with the intention of providing increased sport for Victorian and Edwardian anglers and at the same time it provided employment for those who operated the hatcheries. In fact a very cosy almost symbiotic relationship existed between hatchery operators and their clients. Fishing personas and scientists prominent in the nineteenth century persistently recommended restocking as a way of introducing new blood into a freshwater. They worked hand in glove with hatchery managers promoting stocking as a cure for all fishery ills and it is likely they reaped some financial reward in the process. Sadly and largely unwittingly this practice actually diluted many ancient strains of native Scottish trout, fish which had unique genes built for survival in environmentally different rivers and lochs.

Despite many stock introductions, and contrary to some twenty-first century ill informed opinions, thankfully there are still some pure native Scottish trout populations in existence particularly above impassable waterfalls on a more remote river system, in small isolated burns (streams) and in various large lochs. It should also be remembered that gene dilutions or not, the exceptional quality of Scotland's native trout historically made them of use for stock introductions worldwide. Loch Leven trout were particularly prized as a stocking resource during the colonial times of the late 1800s. Fish culturalists chose the high quality hardy Leven trout above all others as the fish to be exported to such exotic locations as Tasmania, Australia and New Zealand. Trout from the famous Scottish hatchery at Howietown near Stirling were also exported in the latter part of the nineteenth century to such faraway places as Kashmir, Chile and South Africa. Today the trout you fish for in all of these countries are direct descendants of Scottish trout placed there in the late nineteenth century.

The fervour for blanket restocking of Scottish natural waters was to continue apace until the advent of the First and Second World Wars which saw country practices virtually grind to a halt as huge social and economic changes swept the country. Scotsmen in their various regiments were called up to defend their homeland and trout fishing as a sport took a back seat while the country dealt with much more pressing and dangerous issues. At the same time many country estates were split up and sold off in lots with a considerable reduction in the numbers of working staff. As a consequence, one of the first labour intensive practices to go was local hatchery trout rearing. Much of the intensive brown trout restocking practices on estate waters and also various more commercial fisheries ceased or continued in a much reduced form. By the 1970s only the most tightly run native trout farm enterprises continued. Fish culture became an exact business rather than a hobby and, for trout restocking purposes in areas of high demand, the faster growing rainbow trout took precedence.

The Relationship Between Salmon and Trout Fishing in Scotland

Ever since the popularity of sport fishing took off in the nineteenth century, the on-going relationship between trout and salmon has always been a difficult one to fathom. Despite the trout being a quarry much prized by generations of anglers, in Scotland its intrinsic worth has been generally ignored in favour of the much more lucrative salmon. While sea trout became classed as a migratory fish like salmon and therefore have enjoyed all the legal protection provided under the various Salmon Acts which commenced in the 1800s, it was not until the early 1900s that brown trout in Scotland had a legally enforced close season from 6th October to 15th March the following year. Actually while this appears on the surface to have given sea trout a better chance of survival, in practice it has not made a huge difference to its long term existence. Scottish sea trout stocks have suffered greatly from environmental change in the latter half of the twentieth century notably from pollution from fish farms. It should also be noted that the legal classing of sea trout on a par with salmon actually influenced the techniques used in fishing for them. Early sea trout fishing in Scotland was so much like salmon angling it appeared as one and the same thing. Sadly though sea and brown trout are now classed as one species, Scottish law has not been reformed to account for this new classification.

Where migratory and non-migratory trout co-existed in the same freshwater system, the management of brown trout would not be encouraged as salmon fishing was and still is the money generator in Scotland; throughout history trout have been viewed as having very little economic value. Brown trout would often be removed or culled from rivers in the belief that they displaced salmon from their spawning redds and devoured newly laid salmon eggs. Sadly even in the present century, the practice of removing river trout still continues on certain streams in Scotland. Since both game fish species have happily co-existed since post Ice Age colonisation this is a somewhat misplaced theory which some would say is more designed to prevent trout fishers from accessing major salmon rivers. If the trout are 'removed' the angler cannot expect to fish for them. The only river which has bucked this unwritten law is the River Tweed which has had a holistic approach to managing all of its fish populations including brown trout on a largely equal footing since the mid 1800s (see Cornerstones of Scottish Trout Fishing page 56).

Under Scottish law when you fish for salmon on a Scottish river, a permit giving access must be purchased in advance and you will be expected to fish by the prescribed method. Failure to obtain permission to fish and use the right method can result in a prosecution in the courts. Having the back-up of criminal law has assisted in the long term conservation of migratory fish somewhat though Scottish salmon themselves now face huge threats from over-exploitation and habitat change. By comparison the brown trout has had very little sound legal help. Scant protection enshrined in civil law and vaguely tagged on to salmon legislation has meant the brown trout has been over fished near many of the main centres of conurbation. The River Clyde near Glasgow for example, relies totally on stocked brown trout to maintain its fishings. Even as I write in 2005 the law regarding brown trout fishing remains an outdated cumbersome piece of legislation few governments can understand never mind reform. While there is a legal system now in place to protect the freshwater systems providing trout habitat from pollution, the law governing the actual fishing for trout remains sketchy and open to misinterpretation. On the plus side 'Protection Orders' are in place in various areas in Scotland and these allow prosecution of illegal methods thus curtailing over-fishing for trout however Protection Orders are not blanket national legal instruments and while one area benefits another can suffer. Anglers using illegal methods face prosecution on protected waters and therefore transfer their dubious skills to other unprotected sites.

Finnock, the young Scottish sea trout

Scottish Brown and Sea Trout in the Twenty-first Century

Despite traumas in the gene pool, industrial pollution, poor legal cover and sometimes deliberate neglect by salmon-interested land and water owners, it is proof of the Scottish brown trout's resilient qualities that it continues to flourish. Given that today the wild brown trout of Scotland must be classed as fish which have reproduced in a wild natural environment, these trout are a wonderful melange, some bright silver and gold while others a deep burnished bronze. All are beautiful speckled sporting fish and can grow to some considerable size. Ferox can attain double figure weights while a good silvery Leven trout can weigh 4lb plus. They continue to be held in great regard by anglers from across the UK and Europe and committed local fishermen and women remain intensely proud of the beauty and strength of Scottish brownies; in some ways their fighting qualities rather mirror the Scots themselves.

It is a tragedy therefore that this state of affairs does not match the equally loved Scottish sea trout. Once so prolific it was impossible to account for its numbers, the sea trout has now dwindled to a shadow of its former glory. While there are still reasonable populations to be found in specific waters notably inland lochs such as the Hebrides, Loch Hope and border rivers like the Annan and Tweed, overall the large populations of migratory trout dotted the length and breadth of Scotland are now much diminished, victims of ecological and environmental neglect and a great loss in terms of sport. Locating the sea trout has become more and more difficult across Scotland however brown trout largely remain readily accessible. As a rule of thumb, anglers can expect the general density of 'wild' brown trout to increase the further north they travel in the country. In waters of the northern highlands and islands for example, trout populations continue apace especially where the natural spawning is of good quality. In the Outer Isles off the northern Scottish mainland there are more lochs than land and most teem with trout. Far from being an endangered species it's more the case of not enough anglers going there to keep numbers at a comfortable level. The brown trout season runs between 15th March and 6th October and sea trout are roughly the same with a six month off season to allow the fish time to spawn and recover their condition.

The American Rainbow in Scotland

Unlike the brown trout, the American rainbow has no such lengthy association with Scotland only being introduced to the country during the late 1800s. The main reason for its use as a stocked fish was then as always, to increase sport for the angler. The rainbow was viewed as a less dour, more avid feeding fish, keen to devour anglers' flies in most situations and its inherently greedy nature meant it was often less cautious and more easily caught than the canny brown trout. Initially in the late nineteenth century only small private fisheries took on stocks of rainbows as at first the appeal of this fish remained behind that of the native brown trout. However in the latter half of the twentieth century the popularity of rainbow trout fishing took a dramatic and sustained upturn. A rapidly growing leisure market meant many more anglers and, particularly across the central belt, numerous small stocked lochs and ponds were created purely as commercially orientated rainbow fisheries to keep up with the growing demand for easily accessible facilities for trout angling.

Scottish stillwater fishing

Economically by the 1960s many brown trout hatcheries were being found to be unprofitable while the hatcheries concentrating on the faster growing easier managed rainbow were still proving viable. From the late 1970s onward diversification schemes in agriculture meant that farmers could obtain grants to establish both rainbow fisheries and hatcheries on their riparian own inland waters. Almost overnight a rash of commercial small loch/reservoir/pond fisheries sprang up across central Scotland providing farmers with a new and relatively steady source of income. Happily for them the obliging rainbow trout was seen as the ideal fish to meet many Scottish anglers' needs, why bother with the fickle wild brown which was harder to grow and could prove a much more taxing quarry.

By the mid 1980s numerous small commercially run fisheries had effectively taken the place of wild trout waters, many of these being artificially created from reservoirs or by flooding old quarries or mine workings. Unfortunately not all these ponds were run to a high standard with the quality of introduced fish often on the low side and stocking densities far too high for a small acreage of water. This led to some very poor quality fish being caught and effectively created a false impression of what the Scottish trout is all about. For children it was easy to assume that by going fishing for stockies with flabby flanks, dull colour, damaged fins and shredded tails that all of Scotland's trout looked that way. Nothing could be further from the truth. Thankfully through the 1990s there was something of a reversal of this unsatisfactory situation with a gradual improvement of rainbow fisheries standards especially regarding fish culture.

In the twenty-first century modern studies of the rainbow trout in Scotland make interesting reading. In 2002 Dr Andy Walker conducted a major survey of rainbow trout north of the border with fascinating results. If you take it that Scotland has over 35,000 lochs and reservoirs, over 300 of these are stocked with rainbow trout. This may seem a proportionately small number of waters but many other freshwaters may well contain unreported rainbow stocks particularly those on private estates and in rivers where unwanted escapees from fish farms have entered the system. At least fifty-four Scottish rivers contain rainbows which were not deliberately stocked but fortunately the fish fail to breed with any great success in the wild. Both the annual stocking densities per hectare and the average size of introduced rainbows have increased since the last survey of this nature was done in 1974.

Though rainbow trout fisheries are comparatively few in number in Scotland when compared to 'wild' systems they are an important economic and recreational resource and they are extremely popular with many trout anglers from city areas. They offer easily accessed sport with the chance of a large stock fish with perhaps less effort than spending days on a remote loch with the browns proving hard to get. In this respect the rainbow trout fishery has two important roles to play. The first is in taking the pressure off Scotland's wild fish so that rather ironically, the hand-reared pellet fed stew pond rainbow has an important role in conservation. The second is supplying facilities for those anglers who for one reason or another cannot wander along miles of river bank or make it up to the wild mountainous regions to fish for hill loch trout. Fisher folk who cannot get themselves to the true wild fishing of Scotland can therefore still enjoy some form of angling in the stocked fisheries. It may not have the same ethereal appeal but it's still a bit of restorative fishing.

The rainbow trout has no close season in Scotland and technically you can fish for them all year. However, in practice a good many of the small fisheries close for a period in midwinter for maintenance purposes.

Chapter 2

SCOTTISH TROUT FISHING

Earliest Methods

The skill of fishing has existed in Scotland since the earliest of times. In the beginning the purpose of catching trout was almost certainly to render food for the local community rather than to provide sport for anglers per se. Pre the Industrial Revolution which ran from roughly the mid 1700s to late 1800s salmon, sea trout and brown trout were extremely profuse in Scottish rivers and lochs and these fish where easily accessible providing the local inhabitants with excellent nourishment. We know that trout would have been caught by a range of methods prior to rod and line and these included amongst others nets, various traps, otter boards and night lines. Nets would be similar to those used in the sea and they were often strung between narrow banks, across rivers or dragged between two boats or from a single boat with the trout unceremoniously hauled in. A prime example of trout netting was the famous fly water of Loch Leven at Kinross near Edinburgh which was regularly netted up until the 1870s. The trout extracted from Leven where then used as a food supply for the local population. Nets placed at river mouths were almost always for the extraction of salmon with any trout caught in them being regarded as a by catch.

From the eighteenth to the early twentieth century, an assortment of traps principally used for extracting salmon, were also in use on river pools. These included 'baskets' made from woven wood/wicker which would be placed in the river at strategic points often under falls, and into which the fish would fall as they leapt upstream. Though salmon were the main quarry undoubtedly many larger sea trout were taken in this way. Another type of trap used was the 'cruive' akin to the Welsh weir again mainly for the capture of salmon. These were a series of wooden stakes placed in the stream to form an impenetrable cage into which the fish would swim and become trapped. It would also appear that makeshift dams were sometimes used across rivers to trap fish in a pool and that locals would then spear or 'leister' fish out. Salmon would be extracted this way but large trout would obviously have suffered. Equally nasty was 'burning the water' which involved tipping inflammable oil on the water surface and then setting it alight. Fish below would suffocate from the lack of oxygen and trout and salmon would then be easily removed as they floated up to the surface.

Another dubious fishing method was the otter board, a particularly fearsome means of extracting trout, which was outlawed in Scotland in the latter half of the nineteenth century but is still occasionally seen in illegal use today. This consisted of pieces of wood with hooks attached floated out into or across a water system. The 'otter' would sit there with its line of baited hooks attached, a method of fishing akin to the long lining method of England. It would be anchored by twine on to a stake secured on the shore and then left for some time often overnight, before being retrieved usually with several trout impaled on the hooks. Though bait was more commonly used for some reason trout would often take artificial flies attached to an 'otter' more readily than flies cast from a rod and line. Presumably this is because they hang like morsels of natural food suspended in the water column. Similarly night/set lines, now also illegal but still used by the unscrupulous, were composed of a long line with a barrage of hooks or flies attached staked to the edge of river or loch. These would be left overnight and then the catch retrieved surreptitiously under the cover of semi darkness usually just before dawn light.

Before we leave the earliest methods of fishing for trout excluding rod and line I must mention the ancient art of guddling. Trout can be 'guddled' out of small streams especially at spawning time when the fish have thrown their natural caution to the wind so intent are they in the act of procreation. To guddle successfully (though not at spawning time please) you must bodily stand in the stream, reach down to where you know a trout is lying and gently slide your hands under the fish to tickle its belly. The fish is momentarily lulled into a false sense of security whereupon the 'angler' will bring his hands together and whisk the trout up on to the bank. Having attempted this a few times it is not an easy method of fishing if it can be called that, but in the past I have seen others do it with great skill.

Fishing with Rod and Line: Dapping – the First Expertise

Though many may not want to admit it, virtually all forms of rod and line fishing across the UK and Ireland appear to stem originally from angling skills first developed in Europe, particularly the Mediterranean region. Ancient techniques of fishing mimic what we now call dapping, with long rods (sometimes known as Bolognese rods) being employed with flies placed on a single fine fishing line attached to the top of the rod. These long rods have been in use since Roman times, possibly even earlier and are still seen in use today albeit with the addition of a reel. The original Bolognese rod had a flexible loop at the end to which the line was attached. This long rod or pole would then be raised forward above and over the water and the fly or bait not so much cast but dropped or blown on to the surface to try and attract a fish. In effect the technique is dapping by any other name and all testimony to its success for thousands of years later, the long rod is still regularly in use around the sea coasts of the Med.

In Scotland as elsewhere all forms of fly rod angling effectively come from dapping however few early Scottish anglers mention casting techniques per se rather it appears to have been more or less a question of extending the rod at an angle over the water and waiting for the breeze to blow the line and the attached artificial about on the water in a natural way. In the past braided tapered horsehair lines were in use and the wind would billow the line out and the fly would have to be fished as it fell: indeed dapping was sometimes referred to as 'blow line' fishing though this moniker may have come originally from Ireland. In addition to using the artificial fly in this way dapping with a little bunch of live insects such as mayfly or daddy long legs was a popular ploy.

It is interesting that few of the great Scottish pioneering anglers like Stoddart or Stewart of the nineteenth century bothered about writing in detail about dapping. In some way this was not surprising as all fly fishing techniques had partly evolved from the dap and they would probably assume that anglers already understood this concept. In fact greats like Stoddart described in some detail the art of trolling for ferox trout with live or dead bait and completely ignored the gentle more fish friendly dap! Trolling was and still is invariably done by boat with hefty short rods trailing long lines behind them. In the old days the gillie would row his charge around in slow sweeps allowing the bait/lure to swing on a curve which proves highly attractive to any predatory fish lurking below. Nowadays the gillie is often seen as too expensive for ferox fishing and anglers will arrange boat, engine and often an echo sounder between themselves. W C Stewart circa 1850s also fails to mention dapping and instead

Bolognese rods are still in use in Mediterranean regions

discusses using a long rod of 13 to 14ft with silk or horsehair lines while boat fishing on lochs highlighting traditional wet fly technique using multiple flies.

Once shorter, lighter rods came into fashion in Scotland from the late nineteenth century, fly casting methods and fishing techniques became a bit more defined and dapping became a skill detached from other methods of fly fishing. In fact for a time it rather disappeared from native angling literature and it was not until the 1930s and 40s that the skill was mentioned again in any detail. H P Henzell wrote *The Art and Craft of Loch Fishing* in 1937 and then *Fishing for Sea Trout* in 1949. Both these books mention dapping as a successful ploy for trout and in particular the migratory sea trout present in so many of Scotland's lochs at that time and most notably in Loch Maree and the lochs of the Outer Hebrides.

In short, though it seems to have fallen in and out of favour a few times over the centuries dapping has to be recognised as the forerunner of most rod skills in Scottish trout fishing and we shall look further at it in Chapter 4.

Chapter 3

Scottish River Techniques

Fly Rods on the River

Unlike in England where records of trout fishing methods stretch back to the fifteenth century, early details of rod and line methods of river trout angling as a sport in Scotland are extremely scant and only appear to have begun in earnest in the 1800s. Though there are old *Statistical Accounts* of the 1700s which mention men and women going to angle for trout in the lochs and burns of the northern highlands, sport orientated fishing information pre the nineteenth century is very difficult to come by. This is not to say there was no interest in trout, in the 1700s natural historians refer to the fine quality 'red trouts' resident in various highland waters, so there must have been a reasonably well established knowledge of the species though it may have been more concerned with its eating rather than sporting qualities. Incidentally quite how red trout changed to brown trout is now lost in the mists of antiquity, however it is suspected that the determined deliberate anglicising of the Scots Gaelic language from the mid 1700s when 'breac' became 'trout' may have had something to do with it.

In the nineteenth century the landed gentry began to detail their trout fly fishing exploits purely for sport as opposed to a food gathering exercise. Colonel Thornton was one of the earliest writers to describe Scottish rod and line fishing when he wrote his *Sporting Tour* in 1804. In this book he details fly angling with rod and line in what appears to be familiar everyday terms, so it would seem that the art of wielding a fly rod had already been established in Scotland if not much written about well before his time. Happily in the latter half of the 1800s literature concerning Scottish techniques of fly fishing began to appear in more depth. Skills were recorded region by region for example border river trout fishing was considered to bear no relation whatsoever to highland angling despite the fact anglers were all fishing for the same species, wild trout. Techniques specific to a certain river were also placed in print for example trout flies and methods relating to the Tweed, the Clyde or the river Tummel. Though it might all seem a bit futile now, in the past, intense rivalries built up with many a vitriolic exchange written on for example, the effectiveness of a fly or a method local to one region over another. At the core of these arguments would be the elements that go to make up what we now know as …

Traditional Wet Fly Fishing

All of Scottish fly fishing for trout in flowing or still water has essentially grown up around using the wet fly i.e. a fly which sinks a few inches below the surface, the dry fly only arrived in this country toward the end of the nineteenth century almost certainly brought north across the border from the south of England. This use of the wet fly both on river or loch, has been known as 'traditional' fishing for many centuries. The most critical point to remember about traditional trout angling is that this is moving rather than static fishing. Exploration is the key to all traditional Scottish angling, the idea being to cover as many new wild trout territories as possible and in river fishing this means moving up or down the bank between casts on a steady rhythmic progression. The angler who stands solely in the one spot to fish will never be as successful as the peripatetic fisher. In early times, traditional wet fly (or more often flies) would be fished on an essentially 'floating' line constructed of horsehair or later, silk plied with a very long relatively heavy rod maybe 20ft in length. With steady advances in tackle including the introduction of shorter rods, modern reels and the invention of nylon polymer floating and sinking fishing lines, traditional Scottish river trout fishing has evolved into what we know today.

It must be remembered however that though a much greater range of equipment allows the modern angler considerably more flexibility than his peers, the age old techniques of traditional wet fly river fishing have stayed more or less the same over the centuries. Despite modern corruptions of what can be termed traditional angling, notably amongst modern day rainbow trout fishermen who seem to use the term 'traditional' to describe methods only born in the late twentieth century, a team of wet flies fished sunk just below the surface remains the nub of the technique. The flies will be fished on a progression down or upstream on rivers (or for that matter on a boat drift on lochs see page 46), and this method is still accepted as the first river trout angling skill.

To gain a national picture of what we still term traditional fishing it's important to show the diversity of river fly techniques. From the 1800s onward there has been a separation of styles and certain individualistic strands of trout fishing developed across the country to suit particular fishing locales around Scotland. One of the earliest of these techniques was…

'Across and Down' River Fishing

The earliest days of rod and line angling on the trout rivers of Scotland involved little more than a wind assisted perfunctory cast (see dapping) with a wet fly or team of flies across the river after which the angler would make use of the current to drift them downstream toward the waiting trout. This method has forever been termed 'across and down' and it is well etched into the annals of Scottish angling history. It has its roots in early Scottish salmon fishing and its execution is still delightfully simple, only the equipment has been modernised. Teams of wet flies are cast across the river and as they begin to sink the current causes both line and flies to swing round downstream in a gentle arc. The thinking behind this is that the flies will cross the noses of any trout waiting unseen below the water surface and that he will then make a grab for one of the passing apparent pieces of food appearing in his eye line. Once the flies are almost directly below the angler (sometimes referred to as 'on to the dangle') the fisher will lift off and cast across the stream again while at the same time taking one or two steps down river to allow the flies to cover new trout lies. As the flies travel across and down the angler must keep control of them by raising and lowering the rod tip to manoeuvre the line round rocks and through the changing eddies of the stream. In water which is dark with a peat stain, and there are many streams like this in Scotland, this technique works well as the trout are unable to see the angler standing ahead of them. However the technique is not always as successful in very clear water when the anglers' intentions are that much more obvious.

One of the most noted angling doyens of the nineteenth century, Thomas T Stoddart, did a lot to popularise wet fly river fishing using the downstream method. Stoddart (1810 to 1880) wrote two highly successful books, *The Scottish Angler* and the *Anglers Companion to Rivers and Lochs of Scotland*. These brought together skills developed in earlier times and advocated a highly practical approach to wet fly fishing on Scottish streams. He fished

Angling 'across and down'

principally in the border regions of Scotland notably on the Tweed and its tributaries. His technique was basic but skilful using a long softish rod to make a simple switch cast (a type of roll cast) to take the fly across the current and then let the fly line do a controlled drift downstream. Stoddart was essentially a traditionalist but he did not believe that matching the hatch was necessary to catch trout and instead advocated broad brush patterns. Sparse dull coloured flies in shades of black, red and brown hackled with or without a wing were his favourites and these were used as general patterns rather than specific imitations. Oddly enough despite being a Scot, Stoddart had a rather disdainful approach to similar fishing skills which had already been developed in the highlands where across and down was also the favoured method. In particular he was noted for his complete distaste of fishing what we now call attractors, those larger brightly coloured less delicately tied 'gaudy' trout flies which were being used in the more northern parts of Scotland. This might be put done to the social fashions of the mid 1800s which dictated sparse wet fly patterns as *de rigueur*. However despite his sometimes oddly Anglicised views, Stoddart remains an acknowledged pioneer of Scotland's river skills.

33

Using Teams of Flies

It is often assumed that using several flies on the leader is a Scottish ploy purely confined to loch trout angling however in the early days it appears just as popular a traditional wet fly river fishing skill found the length and breadth of Britain. It is not clear if multiple fly angling began as a uniquely Scottish skill which then was adopted nationally or whether it originated elsewhere perhaps Ireland or Wales. Legend has it that a Captain Clarke who fished the Tweed in the early 1800s and may well have stood shoulder to shoulder with Stoddart, was one of the first to use multiple flies on the one tapered (horsehair) leader. His tactic was to tie five or six flies directly into the horsehair line presumably to give himself more chance of catching a fish. Following on from Clarke's experimentation with a school of flies attached, it quickly became common practice across Scotland to use a cast of multiple flies – a method known in border areas as a 'strap'. Often flies would be integrated into the line in considerable number, up to twelve in some cases!

It is not entirely clear when stand out droppers came into common use in Scotland though more than likely it would be when the old tippet materials became more robust, (see also Welsh river angling). Using the multiple fly cast was simply done with the angler starting at the head of a river pool and then taking a few steps down between each cast in the time honoured across and down fashion. Though there are not as many flies on the leader these days, this method is such a relaxed rhythmic style of fishing that it still has numerous devotees not just on Scottish rivers and lochs but across the length and breadth of the UK.

Upstream Wet Fly

Roughly at the same time Stoddart and his contemporaries were advocating traditional across and downstream wet fly angling, another very young border river angler W C Stewart, arrived on the scene. Despite only being in his twenties, Stewart wrote his benchmark Scottish fishing skills book *The Practical Angler* in 1857 and this was to go on to be reprinted no less than sixteen times, certainly a record in terms of Scottish angling books if not nationally. Stewart, like Stoddart, advocated using sparse traditional wet patterns on the river however while Stoddart generally promoted the across and down technique, Stewart plumped for a more exact method in fishing the wet fly 'always upstream'. Not only did he advocate angling upstream but he also devised a set of patterns to be used with this technique (see Stewart's Spider Patterns).

While we accept Stewart's ideas as commonplace now, in the 1850s his departure from mainstream 'across and down' was considered quite radical. He stoutly disputed the success rates of the traditional art of Scottish angling and instead advocated casting an upstream wet fly as the only way to fish. He gave the simple reasons of angler concealment and a more natural presentation as the requirements for using this technique of casting up ahead of the trout. Although upstream fishing had been expounded as early as the seventeenth century by Colonel Venables (see England page 81) and was popular on north country English rivers, it was Scotland's W C Stewart who can be credited for really putting this technique on the UK's angling map. This style of fishing upstream wet was of course in direct opposition to others being used at that time and Stewart's determined advocacy of the new riled his peers no end. Detractors surfaced and Stewart was forced to exchange heated words over whether it was more effective to fish upstream or down notably with Cholmondeley Pennell (he of the fly the Black Pennell). Pennell wrote in the 1860s that 'In spite of Mr Stewart's able advocacy, most anglers have now arrived at the conclusion that fly fishing upstream always, or even generally, is a mistake in practice.' Stewart ably answered Pennell but such were their sniping letters to one another in *The Field* that the editor had to call a halt to their furious exchanges.

Despite those who questioned him at the time, Stewart's upstream wet fly technique was highly successful and right to the present day many anglers follow his pioneering example. Indeed upstream nymph fishing later popularised by Skues and fundamental to the development of English fly fishing may well have been partly derived from Stewart's earlier theories. Stewart's determined upholding of the upstream rule changed forever the ideology behind Scottish river fishing and infused new blood into the old ways. His methods of fly tying were also highly innovative and he perfected sparse wispy patterns, derivatives of which are still in popular use today.

Stewart's Spider Patterns

It is generally accepted that W C Stewart was the first Scottish angler to advocate soft hackle wispy flies very similar to those already in use in the nineteenth century in northern England (see North Country Wet Fly Fishing). Stewart claimed these patterns imitated a wide variety of drowned insects and nymphs and he gave them the general name 'Spiders' even though they were not necessarily an imitation of this particular insect. Spiders are minimalist wingless flies constructed with a sparse skinny body and normally a soft head hackle made from partridge, cock hackle or starling. They differed considerably from the beefy and bushy flies already in popular use during that period. While palmered flies with their over wound bodies and stiff hackles had the tendency to remain high in the water, Spiders did the opposite by sinking quickly below the surface. Once sunk the flies move with an attractive pulsing motion under the water.

The Brora Ranger tied in sparse 'Spider' style. Many of Stewart's flies had only a wisp of hackle at the head and omitted the palmered body

Stewart had three favourites which he thought suitable for any occasion on the river these being the Dun Spider, Black Spider and Red Spider. Oddly enough though Stoddart sniffed at these flies saying they were simply copies of lightly dressed patterns already in use in northern England, he too advocated sparse flies in these very colours. Stewart would fish these flies upstream on a short line employing a stiff rod of around 12ft in length to manipulate the patterns on a raised rod tip as they drifted back down towards him. The art of using Spiders in this way continues to this day and it is all credit to Stewart for producing such outstandingly successful wingless patterns. Given the stronghold of conventional winged fly downstream fishing of that period he did an outstanding job in breaking the mould.

Clyde Style Fishing

The art of Clyde style fishing probably grew up in parallel to Stewart's Spider fishing and the seemingly endless nineteenth century debates over whether it was better to cast up or down the stream. However in contrast to the fairly copious writings on the latter, the styles of fishing commonly found on the River Clyde at Glasgow received very little literary attention.

The reasons for this remain unclear. Certainly Clyde anglers used a selection of unique upright winged flies usually fished in the traditional across and down method, a perennially popular tactic used by central belt anglers for centuries. Perhaps Clyde style flies were not being fished on the more pukka border rivers like the Tweed and therefore were not considered to be ground breaking enough to be recorded until much later. This is a great pity as it would have added a nice practical balance to some of the pernickety debates on fly construction which occurred during the nineteenth century.

In the end it was more or less left to an obscure writer of the twentieth century, Robert Sharp, to document this essentially Scottish skill. Bert as he was known, was a Clyde fisherman for well over forty years and we can be thankful that he wrote *Let's Fish the Clyde* and *Let's Fish Again* as these books carefully document the keenly developed skills used on this famous river. There was very little in the way of purism attached to Clyde style angling and Sharp clearly showed this in his chatty entertaining writing. If trout were not rising a stick bait (caddis larvae) or stonefly larvae (commonly known locally as a 'gadger') would be impaled upon a small hook and cast across and down using the fly rod. Indeed gadger fishing is still employed by many today and while it may not be a fly on the end of the line it is by no means an easy technique. Gadger fishing requires sensitive hands and an awareness of what is happening sub surface and it is very akin to trotting a worm for grayling.

If feeding trout were visible the angler would use a selection of locally designed wet fly or nymph patterns, dressings which Sharp states were passed down to him via an earlier local Clyde angling wizard Andrew Wilson. The wet fly was fished as it landed upstream or across and its aerodynamic design differed from many of the other nineteenth century patterns. Sharp states 'The exceptional style of dressing Clyde wet flies features a short slim body of tying silk or tying silk dubbed sparsely with fur e.g. mole or hare's ear fur, slim wings in many patterns set upright, and a short hen hackle.' The tying-in of the longish rolled wings at virtual right angles to the shaft of the hook is the main characteristic of most Clyde flies distinguishing them from other wet fly patterns. There are some well known Clyde patterns including the Sand Fly (an imitation of the gravel bed fly) and the Hen Blackie which had the more traditional flat wing along the body. Two classic flies exhibiting the true 'sit up and beg' Clyde style were the Yellow of the Mavis and the Shilfie Tip. The former had a black silk body, black hen head hackle and wings tied upright using a light brown secondary feather from the

36 | *Clyde Flies*

Mavis. What this bird might have been is unknown but in hazarding a guess it might be a thrush of some sort as it produced a feather with a distinct light brown at the base. The Shilfie Tip was very similar with a black silk body, hackle of black hen and a wing set upright made from the secondary feather from the chaffinch which had a pale brown edging to it. The use of a very upright wing is common to the Clyde area but not generally found throughout Scotland. It could be speculated that Clyde anglers were more aware of the effect of wind blowing these feathery creations across the stream. This might or might not suggest a tie-in with the ancient art of dapping, certainly the old Clyde anglers seemed much more aware of the aerodynamics of fly construction.

Sharp is rather sparing in his detailing of how the Clyde wet flies were used. He states that the flies would be used in teams of three or more and cast across and down the stream in the traditional way. However he pointed out that when the flies first alight they float and a trout might take them right away so that initially they would be fished dry. Once the feathers had become wet they would be fished in the usual way with a gentle raising and lowering of the rod tip to give the flies a life-like quality. Sharp laid great importance on watching the end of the line indicating that the flies were generally well sunk, nevertheless the first Clyde style flies were almost certainly fished as they fell i.e. in a highly practical way. This is an echo back to the very early days of fly tying and it could well be that the Clyde fishers were actually using dry fly sometime before it was invented on those Halfordian streams of southern England, perish the thought!

Tummel Flies

If Stewart's spiders were sparse and some Clyde flies equally delicate, flies constructed for the fast flowing River Tummel in Perthshire were almost not there at all! There is a telling illustration at the beginning of Skues' *The Way of a Trout with a Fly* showing the design of a Blue Dun according to the different fly tying schools existing at the beginning of the twentieth century. Not unsurprisingly the Tummel tying is the sparsest of the lot which included Hampshire, Yorkshire, Devon, Tweed and Clyde. However unlike the continuing popularity of the other

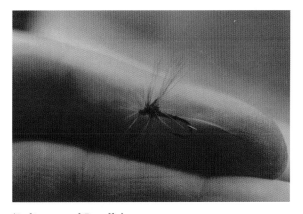

'*Delicate and Deadly*'

contemporaries, the Tummel patterns have almost fallen into disuse. The main reason for this is that the modern angler holds his hands up in horror at the austerity of the dressing. Tummel flies are principally a bare hook with but the tiniest wisp of silk and feather attached. The design dates from the 1800s possibly earlier and it is thought that Tummel flies are a classic example of a traditional fly designed specially for a fast flowing river. Certainly the absence of much dressing would allow the flies to sink quickly in the tumbling clear to slightly peat stained current of the Tummel.

W H Lawrie, a noted Scottish angler of the twentieth century, described Tummel patterns as quick sinking versions of our modern day nymphs and pondered that as long as the fly was the right colour and shape and being fished at the right depth a trout might take it. '*Trout will see what they wish to see*' is a delightful Lawrie description absolutely perfect for the Tummel fly. Certainly the absence of any meat on the fly body seems to indicate a nymph rather than a hatched fly. Again we have an example of an early Scottish fly being designed specifically to cope with local conditions.

Tummel flies were usually fished wet in the traditional across and down manner or cast upstream *à la* Stewart. Though they are not much in favour today they eruditely illustrate the idea that a fly must sink quickly i.e. have good entry into the water, a concept which also runs through river wet fly techniques in England and Wales as well as Scotland.

Specialist Tactics and Flies of the River Tweed

It is interesting that while river wet flies for other Scottish rivers like the Clyde and the Tummel were selectively documented, flies and how to fish them on what must be considered Scotland's principal river the Tweed, were written about in the nineteenth century as if they were to be of use across all of Scotland! This was probably because Scotland's most noted anglers Stewart and Stoddart were both based on the Tweed and therefore it was assumed what they said undoubtedly did for everywhere else. Nevertheless some Tweed fishing nuances did appear during the late 1800s and early 1900s including the tactic of fishing from the 'grey dark to the black dark' a magical time when big sea trout as well as browns will move in close to the bank. Also to be considered are the anglers of old using a 'strap' of flies which would be up to twelve flies knotted into the 'cast' or leader. This forerunner of the droppered cast came directly from the Tweed. These flies would presumably be fished in the traditional wet fly manner of across and down and would certainly have required wind assistance to be effective.

In addition some superb flies came from the anglers who fished the Tweed including the famous Greenwell's Glory, an olive imitation unsurpassed since 1854 and still in frequent use today. This fly was tied by James Wright for Canon Greenwell and was designed to imitate a type of olive (probably the dark olive) commonly found on the Tweed. Its dressing was simplicity itself with wings of blackbird, body of yellow silk, coch y bondhu head hackle with or without a gold rib. The yellow body was well waxed so that it became more olive in nature and though the original fly was wet many Greenwell variants now exist which can be fished dry or wet. It is therefore fitting that we use one of Scotland's best known fly patterns to lead us into…

Dry Fly on Scottish Rivers

While the Scots might lay some claim to pioneering specific river wet fly techniques it would seem that dry fly fishing must have come largely from south of the border. However we must not forget two important points. The first being that Scots anglers did not religiously follow the school of exact dry fly imitation that existed in England from the mid nineteenth century. Stoddart's comments on the finicky antics of his southern dry fly contemporaries 'They give credit to the fish…for possessing a power of discrimination, not less than a degree of daintiness, altogether extraordinary' sum up the Scottish approach to dry fly admirably. The second point to remember is that the Scots were and to a great extent still are, essentially practical anglers not always given to tamely following angling doctrine. This is not so much rebellion against new ideas merely a realist approach to fishing in what can be a wild and rugged country when compared to the tranquil green lawns of the southern chalkstreams. In the early days of river fishing Scottish anglers would have to fish the fly as it fell i.e. if it sank or floated they still fished it out rather than being intent on whether it was fishing as a sunk wet or a dry fly which sat up and begged!

Scots make practical use of the modern dry fly

Historically there is some allusion to various dry fly fishing techniques in Scottish trout fishing. Stoddart described false casting as a means of making the flies 'dry' inferring he had some knowledge of the technique and he also mentioned that a first cast might be successful because the fly floats on the water surface. Stewart propounded on upstream fishing, a noted dry fly tactic, but of course he meant this type of casting to be done with wet fly. For all this, it appears that the Scots got most of their dry fly patterns, if not necessarily all their techniques, from English sources. Few dry fly dressings can be said to be inherently Scottish, however the English took several Scots born flies like the Greenwell's Glory or the Hare Lug (also known in England as the Hare's Ear) and zealously redid the original tyings to come up with dry versions of the old wet flies. From the late 1800s through to roughly the 1940s Scottish anglers largely followed English fly tying trends, however in the latter half of the twentieth century some interesting Scots-led river dry flies became better known. These included patterns like the dry Sand Fly which was a fly hailing originally from the Clyde likewise the Badger and Red, a neat little river dry emanating from the Tweed area.

Looking back it can be seen that most traditional Scottish river dry flies tended not to be over elaborate being fairly minimalist in design yet they are very effective in catching trout. This situation was to continue largely unchanged until the 1970s when a 'new' breed of Scots river angler emerged reviving the old ways and to some extent refining them with the aid of infinitely better rod and line equipment and the employment of many new materials into fly construction. It is perhaps fortunate that the nation as a whole did not take on dry fly fishing with quite the inherent snobbery of their English counterparts and anglers developed a more no-nonsense approach in using the various fly styles for river angling trout. It is good to see that today we use the dry fly across Scotland where the situation calls for it rather than because of any fashion requirement.

Fishing Skills for River Sea Trout

Historically, despite the obvious abundance of sea trout in Scottish streams notably in the many west coast spate rivers and the great east coast rivers like the Spey, Tweed and Ythan, sea trout fishing in Scotland has never been considered a particularly distinct branch of the sport. Salmon were almost always preferred over the migratory trout, indeed in some rivers the migratory trout were classed as a pest along with the resident brown trout, something to be got rid of rather than held in high regard! Thus early tactics for Scottish river sea trout were virtually the same as methods used for salmon with large brightly coloured flies fished fast on floating or sunk lines accounting for many trout. Salmon flies like the Jock Scott, Stoat's Tail or Silver Charm were often used for sea trout although trout flies in large sizes like the Alexandra, Butcher or the Dunkeld were also deemed successful. Pioneering angler R C Bridgett wrote *Sea Trout Fishing* in 1929 and he was one of the first Scots anglers to write in some detail on traditional wet fly techniques for river sea trout. He advocated teams of two or three flies fished in the slow across and down manner on a sunk line and preferred skinny trout patterns fished deep. He also mentions using large black wet flies during the hours of darkness to catch sea trout. Although his techniques could be said to be rather similar to fishing for salmon at least he, unlike many of his contemporaries, made the effort to distinguish methods of angling for the two species.

Sea trout habitat has declined on the west coast of Scotland

From the 1960s onwards and unlike in Wales and northern England which saw specialist skills developing in river sea trout fishing particularly with the Falkus influence, Scotland has largely dragged its heels on devising any new river sea trout techniques. There are a number of reasons for this: the first being that the sea trout specialist has often lost out in that awkward trout versus salmon relationship. In the old days if you went river fishing it was never for trout it was for salmon, the capture of a sea trout was often by accident rather than design. Scottish skills to catch migratory or resident trout never had the kudos of salmon skills. In addition in order to catch good sea trout, dusk and night fishing was and still is an often necessary need. Since salmon poachers operate at night, the innocent sea trout angler was (sadly still is in some quarters) often thought upon as a poacher rather than an expert angler! Finally from the 1960s the overall catches of sea trout began a slow but steady decline which was suddenly greatly accelerated when fish farms were sited in many west coast river estuaries during the 1980s. With sea trout fish not so prevalent many anglers were simply forced into looking elsewhere for their sport. Of course some rivers maintain good runs of sea trout notably along the east and border coastlines but the heady prolific days seem by and large to be gone forever.

Modern Scottish River Fishing

In examining the fly fishing crafts and customs used on rivers from the 1800s if not earlier it becomes apparent that the basic theories of Scottish river trout fishing have not fundamentally changed. Yes in some rivers the character of the fishing has changed slightly in that supplementary stocked trout may have been added or rainbow trout may now be among the indigenous trout populations. In addition some old tactics like using Tummel or Clyde Style flies are less popular now but if you look at the overall picture there has not a huge swing away from the old methods. Twenty-first century Scottish wet, dry and nymph river skills are a delightful mix of past techniques combined with modern equipment and some well designed modern flies. Despite the employment of slow sink, fast sink, intermediate or floating lines in different water heights and lighter stiffer carbon fibre rods (all new inventions from the days when our forefathers fished) by and large river fishing with wet fly is still done in the traditional way. Across and down angling is still immensely popular with a team of three flies. Nymph or spider fishing is still executed upstream or at least up and across rather like the tactics used on the rivers of the northern counties of England and dry fly angling is essentially upstream or up and across with the object to avoid drag i.e. the fly skating around on the surface too fast to give a realistic presentation. Sea trout angling where it can be found is still executed with salmon flies though there has been some adopting of English and Welsh tactics.

Today the adaptable Scottish river angler will use a huge variety of new patterns like CDCs and Elk Hair Sedges easily combined with staunch traditionals like a Greenwell's Glory or a Black Spider and further blended with Americanisms like the Grey Wulff or a well placed Adams. Quite rightly so for the old traditions have easily been woven into the new ideology and add rather than detract from its betterment. The end result works better and it should give us great pleasure to see old traditions upheld and in many cases improved upon.

Loch Ailsh, Sutherland

Chapter 4

Scottish Loch Skills

Early Days on the Loch

In the 1800s the first attempts at Scottish trout loch fishing using rod and line for sport rather than as a means of extracting trout as a foodstuff, appear to have been done mainly by boat often with a gillie at the helm. However it has to be said that a lot of loch angling in the past concentrated on the profuse stocks of salmon and larger sea trout rather the brown trout. There are numerous old paintings from the nineteenth century showing loch fishing in the highlands from a boat but actually these illustrate angling for salmon rather than brownies. However during the course of fishing for salmon, anglers would sometimes encounter large ferox trout which would of course give them a mean tussle well worth recording. Trolling became a particularly popular way of trying to extract large ferox trout from their deep water holds. Bait or spoons (spinning lures) were used particularly on famous Scottish lochs like Rannoch, Ness or Awe, indeed these methods are still employed for ferox on these waters today.

Regarding fly fishing for loch trout in the 1800s it is unfortunate that very few early angling writers bothered to document loch fishing skills when it concerned the humble brownie. While a considerable amount of historical background can be found on early Scottish river trout fishing, recognition of loch angling skills was largely ignored during much of the nineteenth century. This was mainly due to the more eminent anglers of that period (Stewart and Stoddart) deriding loch angling as a largely inferior pastime not much worthy of the gentleman angler. Stewart called it tiresome and monotonous yet obviously he did participate in loch angling as he gave excellent advice on how to do it in *The Practical Angler*. What drove the ancient luminaries to scoff so much at loch expertise is almost certainly linked to a parochial belief that 'their (river) fishing' was undoubtedly superior to anyone else's in Scotland! Their opinions were echoed by English angling masters of the same period. Many across the border had become so obsessed with river angling, fishing upstream and whether to use a dry fly or a nymph, that they completely ignored stillwater skills which were considered inferior as the flies used did not 'match the hatch'.

Dapping

In general despite the fact that forms of dapping with long heavy rods were the forerunner of all Scottish angling skills, the ancient technique was to take something of a back seat in loch methods especially between the 1850s and 1950s when the angling nation went heavily into wet and to a lesser extent dry fly fishing. Dapping became isolated to specific areas like the Hebrides and on larger northern highland lochs such as Maree in Wester Ross. In the 1950s sea trout aficionado Henzell did try and revive an interest in dapping as a technique for lochs, every bit as useful as traditional wet fly.

One of the most detailed descriptions of Scottish dapping technique for brown trout is to be found in the book *Loch Trout* written by Colonel H A Oatts in the 1950s but drawn from at

The author demonstrating dapping at the CLA Game Fair with 15ft rod and floss dapping line

least fifty years of prior fishing. Colonel Oatts was a redoubtable gent complete with plus fours and a mighty Mackintosh to keep out the rain. He lived and fished on the west coast of Scotland in the Argyll area and wrote of using a 14ft cane rod with either a greenheart or split cane top for dapping on the lochs. The blow line (the part of the fly line used for dapping) he used was of floss silk spliced straight on to the backing. Oatts recommended placing a thumb knot in the floss line to stop it fraying too much and to attach the fly he would use about 6ft of gut or nylon. For the novice dapper he thought that a long blow line of 15 yards was easier to work with as it could be easily trimmed to size and the line would be stored on a 4 inch salmon reel. Though he had obviously experienced dapping with live insects, the artificial flies Oatts preferred to use were of the heavily dressed variety with Badgers, Zulus, Black Pennells and Loch Ordie all popular; these patterns are still regularly used in dapping today. Oatts recommended dapping the fly with the rod raised to about 60 degrees with the wind behind carrying the fly in a skittery dance on the water surface. If a trout took he recommended a slight pause before striking to allow the fish to turn down on the fly and this tactic is as much in use today as it was then.

Modern dapping is still done on some northern Scottish lochs with a long rod of 14ft or so and these can be purchased in lightweight telescopic form. The silk or horsehair lines have been replaced either with a light double taper fly line or by using a spinning reel with monofilament acting as the main body of the line. Dapping floss is then attached in much shorter length (about 6ft) and a short length of nylon in the 4 to 6lb range holds the dapping fly which is still of the bushy Palmer ilk with those Badgers and large Loch Ordies size 8 still very popular. A good wind but not a gale remains the best dapping weather and though it is possible to dap from a windblown shore, boat fishing on set drifts with the wind behind is the usual method. Because all that is required is to hold the rod semi upright and let the wind take the fly, dapping is a first choice for a boat angler with little casting skill. Wise old gillies, having sussed out their clients' methods, will often give the dapping rod to the less competent caster.

The dapped fly is said to bring up the larger trout when traditional wet fly fails or is used by one boat angler as an attractor method while his partner fishes a team of smaller wet flies. The idea being that if the trout missed the dap he might snatch the wet fly on the way down – nice thought anyway! It must be cautioned however that the trout must be there in the first place. Drifts must be set along productive shorelines in order to stand any chance of raising a fish. If you compare the catch rates of the dapper over the wet fly angler you will usually find the dapper will lose out from a lack of direct contact with the fish. Trout often somersault over the fly but then try to take it down under the water to drown it. The heavily bouyant fly is whipped up again in the wind and the trout misses its meal. Nevertheless from time to time it is good to mimic the old masters and take a step back into history. Dapping is a lovely easy way of doing just that.

First Loch Flies

Not only did border river aficionados Stewart and Stoddart think that fishing in a highland wilderness was a pretty unskilled pastime when compared with their Scottish borders trouting, they also considered that the flies used for big waters were definitely not of the right design to catch trout. Loch patterns in the nineteenth and early twentieth centuries were considered gauche, gaudy and overdressed indeed Stoddart berated the design of a highland loch fly as 'the latest urban conceit redoubted as a killer'. This was all rather sad as the dressings of wet flies for loch fishing were not quite so haphazard an affair as the doyens imagined. Many of the old traditional flies like the Palmer series are designed to imitate large struggling insects while the Butcher series was used to imitate small darting fish like fleeing sticklebacks. Ranges of flies like the Teal, Woodcock, Mallard or Grouse winged flies were also constructed to imitate insects in their different stages from nymph to winged emerger and not in the slapdash way the past masters of the mid 1850s once suggested.

It is likely just as much thought went into making the old traditional loch flies as it did in designing border river patterns however this was not generally recognised until the twentieth century. Nature is colourful on the lochs with blue damsel flies, red legged bibios, orange bloodworms, bright green beetles, silvery sticklebacks and so on. In making imitations of these natural insects no wonder bright colours were used. The loch fly pedigree is often assumed to spring from patterns designed to be general 'attractors' also known as 'fancy flies' or

The Dunkeld, a possible salmon fly derivative

'gaudy flies' (they are still sometimes given these names) made purely to stimulate an aggressive response from the trout. However a closer look now reveals there was an attempt to match a particular hatch and it is such a pity it was not recognised at the time.

There is also an interesting anomaly in the assumption that the loch patterns Stoddart described as gaudy were derived from brightly coloured salmon flies. It should be remembered that the first Scottish salmon patterns like those detailed by Scrope in the very early 1800s were dull in the extreme. Salmon flies of brilliant hue did not come into being until the brilliantly coloured Kelson versions appeared in England in 1895 by which time Stoddart had died and passed on to higher waters. It would therefore seem that those early loch fly tyers producing brightly coloured patterns in the nineteenth century were doing their best to match the colourful highland hatch and that they deserve considerably more credit than was originally given. The old traditional loch flies were in effect probably devised as patterns suitable for a water habitat containing natural insects and invertebrates of similarly bright coloration and were not merely salmon fly derivatives.

Developing Loch Style Tactics from Boat and Bank

It was only in the late 1800s when club competitions found favour on Scotland's lochs that true loch style techniques began to be taken more seriously. Competitions called for all participating anglers to fish on one water within reasonable sight of one another. Rivers did not lend themselves to this as much as a single large loch where everyone could gather at the pier, set sail in rowing boats and then meet up again at the end of the day for a 'weigh in'. Loch Leven near Edinburgh became the principal national venue for trout fishing competitions and local angling clubs would meet together there to compete, a tradition still maintained today. At first it was very much a gentleman's affair, quite expensive in today's terms and only the wealthier trout anglers took part.

The first tactics were with long trout rods (rods of 14ft plus were commonly used) and horsehair lines dibbling teams or straps of wet flies across the water on a short line in front of the boat. Drifts would be set by the accompanying gillie with the boat moving downwind so that the anglers had their backs to the wind. This allowed both fishermen to work their teams of flies on a medium to fast retrieve and then just before lifting off they would dibble the top dropper on the water surface to attract trout. This technique quickly became known as traditional 'loch style' and it could be practised as much from the boat and the bank. It has not fundamentally changed over the many intervening years. Today you are just as likely to see anglers working flies in the same manner as you would two hundred years ago.

Eventually various successful loch style competitors began to write on how to fish wet fly on lochs. P D Malloch in the early 1900s was an acknowledged expert and wrote a long series of articles on loch style tactics and also a book on the natural history of both trout and salmon entitled *Life History and Habits of the Salmon*. He had his own selection of flies called 'Malloch's Favourites' and these included many well established patterns like the Butcher, Black Pennell, Zulu, Grouse and Claret, Soldier Palmer and so on used on droppers in differing positions largely according to the seasons. Another famous (salmon) angler of the late 1800s William Murdoch also publicised trout loch fishing and gave an interesting selection of his favourite flies including the Green Mantle, the Cinnamon (probably the forerunner of the Cinnamon and Gold) and the White Tip as well as standards like the Zulu and the Mallard and Claret. All modern Scottish anglers must be indebted to Malloch, Murdoch and their contemporaries for leading the way in traditional loch style.

Modern loch competitors follow in the wake of famous anglers like Malloch and Murdoch

Importance of Loch Leven

As Leven has been the centre of competition fishing in Scotland for many years, particularly for anglers based in the central belt, it is worthwhile noting the various fishing nuances which came directly from the anglers fishing this water. We have the 'Leven cast' which consisted of a team of three or more flies tied on droppers on to the main leader which today is made of monofilament but in the past was made of hair or gut. Latterly this would comprise of a make up of traditional patterns like Peter Ross, Teal and Green and the Kingfisher Butcher however today a range of flies might be used with say a dry fly on the top dropper, winged fly mid way and a slim nymph on the point. The Leven cast team of flies would be fished in the traditional manner using the dibble of the top dropper skipped along the surface almost like a dry fly before lift off in order to try and attract following trout. Despite the length of trailing flies none were fished particularly deep, the speed of the retrieve did not lend itself to deeper fishing. The dibbling of the bob fly is a trademark deadly technique for loch style and it is perhaps testimony enough that the skills first popularised on Loch Leven are still highly popular across Scotland in the twenty-first century.

Interestingly Loch Leven also gave its name to a range of flies called Leven Doubles or Wee Doubles. These are heavier traditional patterns made with a double hook rather than a single. Flies like the Dunkeld or the Peter Ross tied on the double hook would often be placed on the point to give the tail fly extra depth and literally pull the droppers down with it. The origin of

47

these flies probably comes from sea trout fishing when small double hooks are used in a safer attempt to capture this free spirited athletic fish. The trout of Loch Leven much resemble the sea trout and this would therefore be the obvious answer to employing these flies. Leven Doubles can still be purchased today and find favour amongst those traditionalist anglers not particularly wanting to use a skinny weighted nymph on their point flies. In addition to devising 'Doubles' modern anglers based on Leven have also given rise to a number of excellent loch patterns one of the most famous being the Leven Spider. With a bright green tail and shiny body this fly is a sure fire hit in the limpid green waters of this enigmatic loch.

And apart from Leven techniques and flies, the Leven trout themselves have played a huge part in the development of trout fishing across Scotland and much further afield. The indigenous trout of Loch Leven were and still are famed for their athleticism and fantastic fighting abilities and in the past were quite literally farmed out world wide. When restocking efforts reached a peak in the late 1800s eyed Leven ova were ferried hither and thither to stock numerous waters from remote Scottish highland lochs to waters in Patagonia or New Zealand! Between tactics, flies and fish, Loch Leven has contributed a huge amount to Scottish fly fishing.

Pioneering the Scottish Loch Nymph

There has been a school of thought that soft hackle Spider fishing devised first for river fishing in the 1850s but later translated to lochs was in effect using a wet fly as a nymph imitation. There is a degree of substance in this theory however because of the historical prejudice which decreed Spider patterns were designed for river use only, few anglers dared fully recognise the importance of nymph patterns in loch fishing. It was not until the early twentieth century that this tactic was better publicised in Scotland. Angling doyen R C Bridgett was genuinely creative in his use of nymph flies in freshwater fishing. Bridgett was essentially a man of the loch rather than the river who wrote of experiences in the early 1900s in a short series of books the most famous of which is *Loch Fishing in Theory and Practice*. Bridgett incorporated both nymphs and dry fly on to his 'cast' (leader) without hesitation or prejudice. His favourites harked back to the Stewart Spiders with sparse body, fine rib and soft head hackles. These were the Black Nymph, Green Nymph, Brown Nymph and Olive Nymph and all are as effective today as they were in the first half of the twentieth century. Bridgett recognised the need for the team of flies to fish at different depths and therefore used the slim wispy nymph rather than a general attractor pattern as a natural imitation often on the tail fly. There is no doubt that Bridgett had taken something of a leaf out of Skues' nymph book as the two illustrious anglers were of roughly the same generation however Bridgett is to be congratulated for applying nymphs to Scottish loch fishing and going where few others had so far dared to fish!

Loch Sea Trout Angling

At one time this subject would have merited a whole chapter if not a complete book! Much was written in the past concerning the vast concentration of excellent loch sea trout angling along the west coast of Scotland. Sea trout abounded in freshwater systems stretching from Dumfries and Galloway along the Argyll coast up to Durness taking in the islands of Skye, Mull and the Inner and Outer Hebrides. From the late 1800s to the 1960s loch sea trout angling was to achieve almost cult status and a goodly amount of literature appeared exclusively concerning Scottish fishing for sea trout. Hamish Stuart wrote *The Book of the Sea Trout* in 1917 and this to some extent paved the way for Scottish techniques for the migratory

loch trout. He was one of the first Scots anglers to draw a definite distinction between salmon and sea trout techniques. He recorded that his most successful tactic was to use teams of small trout wet flies like the Zulu and Mallard and Claret rather than the larger gaudy salmon fly preferred in the 1800s by other angling luminaries of the period. These he would ply with a single handed rod from the boat in traditional loch style fashion.

It must also be remembered that during the heyday of loch sea trout (1890s to 1960s) a considerable amount of sea trout angling was being done not only in freshwater systems but also in the sea lochs (known as voes) indented into the coastline of the Shetland Isles. The techniques required for fishing either in fresh or salt water did not and still today do not differ that much. Most anglers used single handed rods, sunk or floating line with slim line wet trout flies like the Teal Blue and Silver, Dunkeld and/or Butcher. Sometimes small salmon flies with double hooks would be used to add a bit of weight to the cast. Top droppers would be reserved for bushy patterns like the Red Palmer or the Black Zulu. The flies would be fished 'loch style' in teams in saltwater casting out, allowing the point fly to sink and then retrieving the flies back using a reasonably fast retrieve. Just before lift off the top dropper would be dibbled causing a little wake on the water which would hopefully stir the sea trout's curiosity sufficiently enough for him to take one of the flies. This differed quite considerably from the slow swinging across and down techniques of river sea trouting. It could be said that saltwater loch sea trout anglers were probably the first anglers to recognise the need for these migratory fish to have something to chase and therefore used a much faster retrieve than the river norm.

In the 1920s J C Mottram added extra skills to established loch sea trout tactics by advocating dry fly for sea trout in his tome *Sea Trout and Other Fishing Studies*. Later H P Henzell wrote the timeless *Fishing for Sea Trout* in 1949 which again featured wet and dry skills but also 'rediscovered' dapping as an alternative means to using teams of wet fly fishing

Loch sea trout par excellence

to attract fish. In the 1960s Charles McLaren, Jock Scott and W B Currie were probably the last Scottish writers to record loch sea trout techniques in any detail. By then tactics had been rounded together to include dapping (which had come back into vogue), sunk and floating line angling, daylight and night-time techniques and wet and dry fly skills.

Looking back at all these well established techniques for loch sea trout, it quickly becomes obvious that this branch of Scottish angling had developed quite independently of both English and Welsh sea trout techniques. While native brown trout angling has seen a fair amount of external influence over the centuries particularly from England, Scottish sea trout loch fishers had been much less affected and had continued to develop techniques in their own unique way. Sadly today, while loch sea trout skills have not fallen into complete disuse, the opportunities to practise them have declined in tandem with the general decline of Scottish sea trout angling. That is not to say that all Scottish sea trout have disappeared, fish are still caught in various well managed fisheries, but they are considerably less in number and often smaller in size. Climatic change, poor siting of fish farms, netting, over fishing – take your pick. The tactics to fish for sea trout have not been forgotten rather they have been absorbed into the Scottish angling heritage, time moves on I suppose...

Dry Fly on the Loch

Initially the dry fly was thought to have little or no place in loch fishing being considered a fly for river use only. Despite the fact that large bristly palmered flies had been dapped and dibbled over the surface of lochs with the aid of a stiff breeze from at least the early 1800s, this method was dismissed as bearing no relation to 'real' dry fly fishing. In addition the bob fly on a team of wet flies would skip and scutter like a floating dry fly as it was being retrieved. Again this was discounted by the leading nineteenth century authorities as having no likeness to dry fly angling even though the fly would float on the surface.

Thankfully R C Bridgett in the 1920s was all for employing dry fly on the loch, much to the horror of some of his fellow anglers still stuck in the upstream 'dry fly only on rivers' time warp! Bridgett recommended using dry fly when trout were visibly rising to sedge or olive hatches and also when the fish were feeding randomly on the occasional land blown flies like Midge and Black Gnat. In advocating dry fly for loch fishing Bridgett tenaciously flew in the face of convention and should be much admired for stating 'The time has come when the floating fly is a requisite lure for the loch and no angler should delay realising the fact'. Today this ethos is almost universally accepted however these were brave words indeed at that time.

The Scottish Mayfly

Despite the abundant existence of mayfly (Green Drakes) in the northern and western highlands of Scotland this vitally important insect species was, and still is to a certain extent, largely ignored by the bulk of anglers unless they happened to live right in the thick of it. Even the great W C Stewart circa 1850 dismissed mayfly fishing in Scotland as 'hardly deserving attention'. This was because anglers fished the live mayfly as 'bait' on a small hook on certain rivers (Stewart does not specify which) and Stewart found the natural insect was 'as difficult to catch as the trout themselves'. Instead Stewart cites what he termed the mayfly of Tweedside and the border districts which are actually types of stonefly as being the most important in angling terms. Apart from extolling the virtues of the stonefly nymph which he calls the 'Creeper' (also known as the 'Gadger' of the River Clyde), Stewart sadly fails to recognise the importance of the real Scottish bred mayfly i.e. Green Drakes, so prevalent in the far north.

Even in more modern times while many fishers might have heard of the Irish mayfly considerably fewer recognise the mayfly as indigenous to numerous northern lochs particularly those within the counties of Caithness and Sutherland. In addition certain lochs in Wester Ross, Inverness-shire and Argyll also feature a mayfly hatch. Why this lack of recognition should be can only be put down to a lack of understanding of the natural history of the northern parts of Scotland. Too many laymen simply dismiss the far reaches as bleak barren places dominated by mountains, moors and peat bogs. Their arguments are based purely on face value assessments and consequently they ignore the fact that parts of the highlands are extremely rich and fertile in nature. Also because the Caithness/Sutherland mayfly do not begin hatching until mid June, reach a high peak in mid July before tailing off in the latter half of August, the less well informed visitor often assumes these luscious insects do not hatch at all! Later the hatch may be than say on English chalkstream or an Irish lough, but it is no less profuse and often goes on for considerably longer.

The main prerequisite for a successful Green Drake hatch is a good habitat for the burrowing nymph. Caithness in particular has a huge amount of soft clay-like mud called marl and mayflies thrive in this unique environment. Interestingly though the mayfly also do well in making burrows in peat banks and will still hatch profusely given the right conditions. Of the two thousand plus lochs within Sutherland and Caithness very few do not contain mayfly so that's a heck of a lot of top quality fishing. Poor research by naturalists and visiting anglers cannot account for all of the ignorance surrounding the highland mayfly however, the anti loch doctrine of Stewart and Stoddart must also be taken into account. If the doyens virtually wrote off highland waters as hardly worth visiting except to troll for ferox, little wonder the Scottish mayfly remained undiscovered and unwritten about for so long.

Given that mayfly are so numerous you might think that right from the early days a good Scottish designed imitation of the insect might have been constructed. This does not seem to have been the case however. It is quite possible that in the 1800s those big bushy dapping flies like the Loch Ordie, Badger Palmer or Red Palmer were used as non specific but nevertheless very effective patterns as they easily resemble a big mouthful ready for the trout to gobble up. This trend in using general attractor flies during the mayfly hatch continued right through most of the 1900s with few Scottish born patterns emerging if you will pardon the pun. In particular the use of those dainty meticulously tied presentations as devised by the dry fly fraternity in the south of England was virtually unheard of in the far north. Certain Irish imports have become popular as mayfly imitations in the latter half of the last century notably Bumbles, Green Drakes and Dabblers but in general the Scots remained true to the theory that when the trout are feeding well on fat insects the fish will take virtually anything in their path. While the English became obsessed with exact representations of the Ephemera, Scottish anglers carried on fishing their Loch Ordies, Ke Hes and Palmers to great effect during the mayfly hatch.

Scottish mayfly remain greatly underrated

Apart from dapping which may have employed live mayfly as much as a large bushy pattern, tactics for dry fly fishing during the mayfly can take two threads. When the weather is calm a single gently twitched dry fly like a Grey Wulff or a dry March Brown will often take trout busily engaged in enthusiastic feeding. During a good breeze a bushy top dropper like a dry Rough Olive or a Golden Olive Bumble can be tripped through the wave and this will often bring up large trout which thrash at the fly with hefty takes. Whatever your tactic the Scottish mayfly carnival is an event not to be missed under any circumstances.

Fishing for Rainbows in Scotland's Lochs and Reservoirs

The habit of introducing stocked rainbow trout into small lochs and/or reservoirs has been going on for at least a century in Scotland however the popularity of rainbow trout fishing really took off from the 1960s. By the early 1980s numerous small commercial fisheries had sprung up particularly in the central belt and many of these have continued apace. The slow decline of wild natural brown trout stocks in the more populous areas of Scotland has meant many city based anglers now know little else other than rainbow trout fishing. The number of commercial rainbow trout fisheries in Scotland in no way matches those of England however it is true to say a considerable number of Scots anglers now fish more for rainbows than they do the indigenous Scottish brown trout.

Tactics for these fish are much the same as fishing for rainbows in any stocked pond across the country and can involve anything from Buzzers to Tadpoles with Cat's Whiskers and Muddlers also in there with a shout. These flies, which are largely English imports, will be fished on anything from a floating line to a Hi D (heavy sinking line) with plenty of use being made of the intermediate as well. The only slight difference in fishing for Scottish rainbows is that traditional habits die hard and a fair number of fishers still fish with customary loch style much in the same way they angle for brown trout. Thankfully the rainbow trout respond well to the old tactics except when intent on sulking near the bottom. For further extensive notes on universal rainbow tactics see English Lake Fishing page 103.

Modern Loch Angling – Tactics and Flies

It is important to remember that traditional loch style is still a highly popular skill with its roots in Scottish wild trout angling going back over roughly two centuries. The essential skill remains in using a team of wet flies on a short floating line cast in front of the angler who has his back to the wind. These flies are retrieved back at medium pace with a dibble of the top dropper before lifting off. While it is recognised as a wet fly skill the flies are not fished at great depth, anything from 6 inches to about 2ft below the water surface is the norm, and the flies are kept in motion by a fairly fast retrieve. Traditionally this will be done from a boat but it is just as effective from the bank for both migratory trout and resident browns. Today in the UK you will find various corruptions of this 'top of the water' technique with anglers fishing an English reservoir for rainbow trout with heavy lures and/or nymphs on deeply sunk lines and calling this tactic 'Loch Style'. These bear little resemblance to real Scottish brown trout loch angling and are merely other methods of stillwater fishing. Of course modern loch anglers benefit from a much wider range of technology at their disposal including high quality carbon fibre rods capable of launching the fly many yards if necessary and also a range of fly lines able to take the fly to any depth in the blink of an eye. Nevertheless the execution of true loch style has not changed that much.

What have altered quite dramatically are the types of flies seen in use today on Scottish lochs. There has been a huge expansion in the range of patterns now considered suitable for big waters. Scotland's twenty-first century loch patterns tend to fall into two categories. North of the central belt the majority of modern loch flies remain true to their roots. Though the flies may be constructed with newer materials like deer hair (as in the case of Muddlers), holographic tinsel, fluorescent wool, sparkling chenille and so on, the shape and overall design has not altered that much over the last two hundred years. There are still Palmers, Spiders, Nymphs and numerous winged patterns in common use north of say Perth. However because a good numbers of anglers in the central and southern reaches of Scotland now fish for rainbow trout (even the famous Loch Leven is now a put and take fishery) loch fly design in this region has encompassed more of the bright colours and marabou materials associated with catching this type of trout. Thus trout fishers in the central belt use a wider variety of patterns taking in both brown trout traditionals alongside largely English sourced flies like the Ace of Spades, Boobies and the Dog Nobbler.

Today loch flies are unbelievably numerous and this can largely be put down to the stillwater anglers' influence. Anglers fishing for rainbow trout have introduced many new patterns into traditional brown trout loch fishing. Some of these have proved very successful, some not. Of course traditional patterns like the Grouse and Claret or the Soldier Palmer are still in use on the lochs but now you are just as likely to see anglers using anything from ultra modern Buzzer variants to Black Marabous or Cat's Whiskers. In addition dry fly, nymph and wet are all used in happy tandem so much so it is not uncommon to find them all as droppers on the same leader. For example a dry fly might be the top dropper, a traditional wet mid dropper and a nymph on the point. In this respect Scottish loch angling has become supremely flexible in its approach and in doing so has advanced considerably. Old prejudices of the 1800s are now forgotten and a good thing too!

The modern fisher's fly box

Chapter 5

CORNERSTONES OF SCOTTISH TROUT FISHING

In order to gain a realistic picture of what Scottish trout angling has become we have been taking a step back and looking at how the differing technical strands of fishing have evolved. In doing so it has quickly become obvious that the advancement of Scottish trout fishing has never followed the easiest of paths. Thankfully we have come a long way from the social divisions and snobberies that dominated our loch and river fishing in the past but it has been a long haul. Even as late as the 1950s fishing writers were dismissing loch fishing as an inferior sport. Pat Castle, writing in the 1920s in his book *Trout and How to Catch Them*, stated 'Fishing a loch from a boat is far removed from the real thing and the fishers who have only angled in this way know very little about angling.' Such pompous statements tellingly illustrate that old prejudices born in the mid to late 1800s took a very long time to die. Fortunately most of the extraordinary narrow mindedness which pervaded sections of Scottish angling for far too long has now gone.

In addition important moves to conserve Scotland's native brown trout have been assisted by the comparatively recent advent of Protection Orders (late twentieth century) which are enforceable laws covering all fish species within a river or loch system. The legal side of conserving the wild brown trout, always a grey area, has been aided by these POs, their only drawback being that they cover specific areas rather than the whole of Scotland. We have also embraced rainbow trout fishing into our heartland and these fish must be recognised as an important leisure asset. Though the American interlopers may cause some unrealistic expectations of the size of Scottish trout especially amongst young anglers, they serve a useful conservation purpose in taking angling pressure off wild fish.

Now follows the difficult task of giving you a few examples of waters which show best how the old skills and techniques already described have grown and evolved over the years. In doing this please remember it is not my intention to give you guidebook style 'where to go' information. There is plenty of that elsewhere, some of it written by me, some not. Instead this chapter concentrates solely on a few select cornerstones, waters where local anglers have nourished essentially Scottish techniques right from earliest beginnings and these are still going strong. Suffice to say most of Scotland's wild trout fishing is always worth a visit and after a somewhat sticky start, most of this country's rainbow trout fisheries are now much improved in quality. And remember that if you want a more detailed view on Scotland's rivers and lochs you can always buy a copy of my book *Scotland's Classic Wild Trout Waters* also published by Swan Hill Press.

A Premier River – The Tweed

There are many excellent brown trout rivers in Scotland including the Don, Tummel, Tay, Spey, Clyde and Annan but the one with the longest and most illustrious history has to be the

Tweed. This was the stomping ground of not only Scottish angling pioneers like Stewart and Stoddart but also famed salmon specialists like Scrope and Younger. It is home to famous trout flies like the Greenwell's Glory and Scrope's dowdy but effective salmon flies and it is here that many river fishing techniques with Victorian tackle were first tried tested and honed. Many of these skills were adopted nationally, (see also Special Tactics and Flies of the River Tweed page 37) and the river has remained a hugely popular trout fishing venue for well over two hundred years with salmon angling records going back as far as the seventeenth century.

However the critical factor which places the Tweed above its other watery peers is its unique management system which still is the only one of its kind in Scotland. It is testimony enough that today the quality of the Tweed's trout can easily match the quality of trout caught in the 1800s. Fish management on the Tweed has been established since 1857 when the River Tweed Commissioners, drawn from representatives of riparian owners, local authorities, angling clubs and other interested parties from both sides of the border (the Tweed has approx twenty-three miles of its ninety-eight mile length in England), took it upon themselves to work toward 'the general preservation and increase of salmon, trout and other freshwater fish in the River Tweed and its tributaries'. The key words in this impressive mission statement were 'trout and other freshwater fish' as this meant that all fish populations were to be managed on a reasonably equal footing. Most Scottish rivers then and now manage their fish populations with a view to protecting money-generating salmon first with other less valuable stock fish like trout given little or no long term investment or habitat attention.

In 1983 these ground-breaking fishery management aims were further taken up by the Tweed Foundation and with eminent fisheries biologist Ron Campbell at the scientific helm it has gone from strength to strength. The Tweed Foundation philosophy is a supremely holistic one. They believe that at the end of the day, successful fisheries management has little to do with actually managing the fish – they are pretty good at that themselves if you give them a chance – it is more about managing people and the effects they have on fish. It is not surprising that the Tweed remains the principal example of good practice in river management certainly in Scotland if not throughout the UK. Few other Scottish rivers show the same degree of commitment in managing ALL fish species on such a sound well informed scientific basis. Statistically the Tweed produces more fish caught to the fly than any other river in Britain, testimony enough to its exceptional far sighted management.

The trout fishing on the Tweed is largely controlled by local angling clubs and features a number of innovative fishing tools including the issuing of brown trout fishing diaries to regular Tweed fishers. These record in comprehensive detail the numbers of trout caught and/or returned, the time spent in doing so (fishing effort), the size and markings on the trout, places visited, river condition, the weather and the number of other anglers on the water that day. At the end of each season this information is collated and the information gathered helps in making future management decisions on for example the need to improve habitat or to restock a section of the river.

It is interesting that policies are constantly evolving over trout restocking on the Tweed. During the mid 1900s it was commonplace to stock feeder burns with fry but this practice was halted when the scientists of the Tweed Foundation conducted surveys of the burns and found them already well stocked with native trout fry. It was felt that the practice of adding new fry simply wasted resources as the introduced fry caused excessive competition and stress amongst existing fish populations.

In addition any new stockie trout introductions are now marked with a blue dot to

River Tweed

distinguish them from the wild population. Anglers are allowed if they wish to kill the dotted trout but are actively encouraged to put back unmarked fish as these are the native trout of the Tweed system. It is recognised by most fishers that it is vital that the Tweed strain of trout continues to flourish as it is totally one of a kind. Ron Campbell and his team have also discovered that the river has the highest rate of trout/salmon hybrids in Europe. Tweed trout show a higher than normal degree of mobility within the river system and this has been put down to a mixing of salmon and trout genes at the spawning redds. Indeed the native trout have been shown to have a 20 per cent salmon gene and Tweed sea trout can grow as large as salmon and some brown trout err more on the size of small grilse. Again this is down to accidental genetic mixing at spawning time.

Fishing for trout on the River Tweed is a real pleasure even if you do chance upon a stockie rather than a wild one. The environment is superb with rich vegetation, huge insect variety and stunning wildlife. The water is clear with an alkaline pH and in many ways the river resembles a larger version of a Hampshire chalkstream as the base is of gravel and the crystalline flow is woven with excellent beds of ranaculus. It is even more impressive if you think that the Tweed is actually a recovered river rather than a pristine one. During the Tweed fabric mills industry boom of the late nineteenth century the river became so polluted with clothing dye that little if anything could survive in it. Thankfully the riparian owners and Tweed Commissioners won the day and the industrialists were forced to back down over discharges into the river but for a time it was touch and go whether any fish would survive at all in the lower more populated reaches.

Today most Tweed trout aficionados go for light tackle and fine leaders. Dull breezy days tend to be more productive than sunny conditions and dusk fishing is often favoured due to the clarity of the water. Sea trout are still present in some number and dusk to dark is a good time to try for them using old traditional patterns like the Cinnamon and Gold or the Invicta

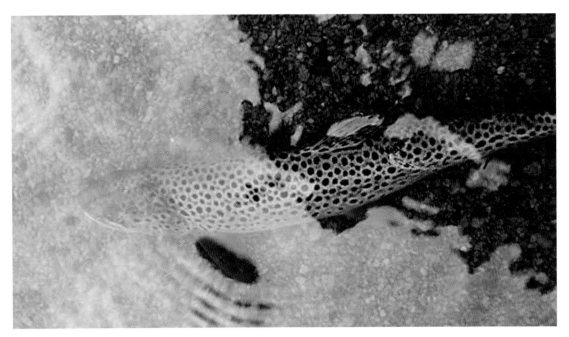

Tweed trout have twenty per cent salmon gene

or go modern and use one of Hugh Falkus's flies like the Secret Weapon as they do on those gin clear Welsh rivers. If you want a greater chance of native rather than stocked fish keep away from the town waters such as Galashiels or Peebles as these are stocked. Remember the native trout are likely to be small as there is prolific natural spawning on the Tweed. Ancient records of huge bags of trout must be tempered by the fact that the anglers of old killed everything in sight from a 3oz trout to a 3lb one! Nevertheless there are still leviathan trout in the Tweed and you will need stealth and cunning to tempt them. Modern Tweed anglers will use a combination of the old wet flies like Spiders, Greenwell's, Snipe and Purple and Partridge and Orange with newer patterns like CDCs, Iron Blues and Sedge patterns. Nymph fishing can be very productive in cold high water with Pheasant Tail and Stonefly nymphs popular. Choose your rod and line according to water height but in general terms the lighter the tackle the more subtle you can be in attracting those marvellous Tweed trout. This river shouts respect and I can't say more than that…

Loch Watten – The New Loch Leven

As we have already learned, Loch Leven was at one time the principal wild trout fishery of Scotland. Its trout could not be bettered for quality and athletic ability. The fact that it sustained competition fishing for over one hundred years without difficulty shows that this place was and to a degree still is something special. Sadly during the latter half of the 1990s eutrophication of Leven became so great that the traditional brown trout angling suffered dramatically. In a bid to retain anglers for commercial reasons, American rainbows were introduced into the loch and today Leven is known as much if not more for its rainbow trout fishing than it is for its wonderful browns. Some anglers see this as moving with the times while others, myself included, feel deeply saddened by the loss of an irreplaceable heritage. Stocked rainbows grown in tanks are ten a penny, native Leven trout which colonised the loch after the last Ice Age are priceless.

As a consequence of the changing fortunes of Leven we must look further north to find exceptional wild trout fishing on lochs of reasonable size. Loch Watten in Caithness is just such a venue and many believe it has now taken the place of Leven as one of the premier wild trout fisheries in Scotland. If not the best wild fishing in the country it comes inordinately close. Interestingly both waters have similar parallel histories in that Loch Leven was once the preserve of the well heeled angler in the latter part of the nineteenth century. Equally Loch Watten was fished for a time almost exclusively by the wealthy being part of the Duke of Portland's estate. Fishing in the early days was largely preserved for the local landowners and their guests. Despite his apparent disdain of all things highland Thomas Tod Stoddart visited Loch Watten in 1851 describing it as having 'excellent trouting during the summer and autumn months'. Stoddart remarked on some of the Watten trout 'resembling in every respect small sea trout'. This characteristic he noted was also found in silvery trout native to what he describes as the 'Compensation Pond' near Edinburgh and though he does not stipulate, the colour and markings must have been extremely similar to the trout of Leven.

The indigenous trout of both Watten and Leven are very alike being of streamlined torpedo shape with beautiful silver and gold flanks and supreme athletic ability. Both fish populations show a roving almost pelagic lifestyle given to travelling at speed upwind to hunt down aquatic prey like sea trout. Old rumours have it that this is more than a coincidence and that in the past Leven trout were used to stock Watten or that Watten trout stocked Leven depending on which piece of history you believe! Personally I feel it is likely that during the Victorian mania for restocking waters whether they needed it or not, Watten would indeed have seen some

Watten success

Leven trout introduced into it. However without genetic sampling it is extremely difficult to tell how much this affected the genetic line of native Watten fish, very little I suspect as this northern trout population has generally thrived with good access to the local spawning burns.

The most plausible reason for the similarities between Watten and Leven trout is the considerable likeness of the respective habitats of the fish. Both lochs are rich aquatic environments, clear, shallow and alkaline in nature with good weed growth. For centuries trout thrived in the clear waters of each loch however while Watten has remained virtually unchanged, Loch Leven has undergone dramatic swings in water quality. Over enrichment of Leven has been its bugbear since the 1980s though even before that the loch could see erratic fluctuations with algal blooms clouding the water to such an extent the fishing would change in character. Instead of the wonderful traditions of top of the water fishing with floating line and a team of wet flies, Leven anglers were forced into using heavy sinking lines and lures to attract fish which rarely rose and for the most part seemed to hug the bottom of the loch. Introducing rainbow trout with all their very different associated lure fishing techniques was the final straw for some traditionalists.

Thankfully when fishing Watten today the angler can still employ a variety of time-honoured loch skills to the full while blending in some newer techniques if the conditions demand. With a good breeze the trout of Watten respond well to that first expertise dapping, especially during a warm June or July when trout are near the surface ready to pounce on any tasty terrestrial morsel coming off the surrounding farmland. Loch Ordies and Black Palmers do well on the dap and these patterns work equally efficiently in traditional wet fly mode.

Fabulous Watten trout

Today most Watten regulars plump for floating line and teams of smaller wet flies size 10 to 14 in amongst many the Bumble, Black Pennell, Rough Olive and Greenwell's Glory style. These flies are fished predominantly from the boat on a short line with a fast retrieve and takes are firm and fast. As Watten is comparatively shallow throughout its three mile length, fish can be caught across most of the water though early and late in the season drifts parallel to the bank where you can still see the bottom are highly productive. Natural insect and invertebrate life is prolific with high density Black Gnat, Olive, Caenis, Midge and Sedge hatches. Mayfly are found here and there where there are patches of marl, however it is interesting that they are not as prolific as on some of the smaller Caithness waters like St Johns or Toftingall. Shrimp and snail are also abundant on Watten and trout grow sleek and fat on a good quality diet of crustaceans.

Anglers fishing Watten must adapt quickly to the changing conditions of this exposed water. Just like Leven it has never been a beginner's loch and you need to keep your wits about you at all times. Of particular relevance is the fact that Watten trout exhibit roving tendencies just like their Leven compatriots. Often when there is a good hatch on they will appear to travel fast upwind gobbling down insects as they go. To this end a dry fly placed in a feeding fish's path will often be vigorously seized and Hoppers, Grey Wulff and Red Sedges fished dry will produce the goods. Dry fly is also good in calm weather though it takes a steady hand not to strike too soon as a big silvery trout suddenly rises and rolls over the fly before taking it underneath the surface. Though they are not necessarily the first choice for local anglers, a team of small nymphs like the Hare's Ear or Black Buzzers will take trout which seem to be ignoring traditional wet fly.

Loch Watten therefore is perhaps the new preferred home of traditional loch style. Further to travel it may be but the rewards are far greater for the angler who enjoys a significant brown trout challenge. Fish it and close your eyes for a moment. It is not hard to imagine how Loch Leven once fished, some call Watten the 'new' Mecca for loch style fishing. It is a title it richly deserves…

Fishing the Gaudy Fly in Lewis

There are a number of claimed original homes for the 'Traditional' or 'Gaudy Fly'. These mainly feature along the west coast and the northern highlands of Scotland. Basically any pattern tied with a shimmer of tinsel and a splash of colour can be called a Gaudy Fly. These patterns so berated by the Scots angling doyens of old like W C Stewart or Stoddart for being too bright and unlike any natural insect, remain powerful trout attractors perhaps even more popular today than they were in the 1800s. Usually they are fished on a floating line in teams of two or three flies. The retrieve is fast to make the flies resemble small fleeing fish or fast escaping insects. Because of their brighter flashier hue the flies are effective in dark peaty water and they are also thought to better attract migratory fish like sea trout.

It is fitting therefore to use the Hebridean Isle of Lewis as a classic example of where these generic patterns do best. Lewis is pitted with a huge diversity of timeless lochs ranging from moorland to machair and from dark peat-stained waters to limpid transparent pools. Most contain game fish ranging from a few ounces to several pounds in weight. The island is a place steeped in history where fishing has grown up hand in hand with a unique practical crofting lifestyle. Living in an often harsh wild landscape, trout, sea trout and salmon have been an important source of food to crofters who as well as using fly would use net, worm or spinning tackle to catch their fish. While today this might be frowned upon it must be remembered that in the past freshwater fish were an important food supplement rather than a recreational plaything. Fishing methods were therefore quick and practical rather than an art form. Today however local and visiting anglers fish more for pleasure and sport than they do out of necessity. The trout remain ecologically the same; it is only the society around them which has changed.

Few fly fishers use anything else other than Butchers, Peter Ross, Silver Invicta, Alexandra, Dunkeld or the Worm Fly to name but some of the popular traditional patterns. These will usually be used in sizes 10 to 14 on 4lb to 6lb tippets as you never quite know when you might connect with a big 'un. The order in which the flies appear on the leader is important. Often anglers will use them in the 'chasing fish' combination. This means a shiny fish like fly like the Butcher or the Dunkeld will be placed on the tail or point fly and a larger more bushy bob fly like a Black Zulu will be placed above it. It is thought that by using a medium to fast pace retrieve the flies look like a tiny fish chasing a large morsel of prey and that a big trout or sea trout will eventually dash in to seize the 'prey' or for that matter the 'competition' before the little fish reaches its target. This theory may sound a bit airy fairy but in actual fact nine times out of ten this fly combination does just that especially with sea trout present. Sea trout like to chase their prey of sand eels and/or small fish down and therefore a flashy sparkly lure looks all the world to them like a small fish. Remember sea trout and brown trout are the same species and spawn in similar habitats. There will be an intermingling of genes intentional or unintentional and therefore trout populations with some access to the sea as on Lewis will often exhibit this highly active 'chase the prey' tendency.

Anglers on Lewis fish from either boat or bank with equal success. Working along a shoreline with traditional patterns you can expect to pick up spanking bright trout especially

Timeless loch fishing on Lewis

Typical gaudy flies for Lewis

during the months of April, May and June when large trout linger near the margins and casting a long line is not necessary. Depending on the nature of the loch(s) you fish, darker peaty waters on the west of Lewis clear and quite rich on the east side, a degree of stealth will be involved. However it has to be said that as many waters are under rather than over fished the tactics are fairly simple on a short line and fast retrieve. A number of lochs have boats accessed either through the local angling Association or through estate offices but going afloat is not a prerequisite for capturing large trout, bank fishing is just as good. And as you hook into that first wild trout of the day remember that you are fishing as generations have done before you. The sense of place here is intense, Stewart and Stoddart pioneered much in Scottish angling but they did not do everything. Casting your Gaudy flies in silent remote waters it's good to think that highland anglers also knew a thing or two about attracting trout...

Mayfly in Sutherland

Green Drakes thrive in the wilds of Sutherland despite a landscape which looks so harsh that it is often assumed nothing can survive long there. This northern county of Scotland has some two thousand plus lochs and lochans and there are actually very few which do not contain at least a few mayfly. It is interesting however that despite the prolific hatches of this important insect few exact representations have been devised locally. While the English mayfly devotees created works of art *à la* Halford the main tactic for highland mayfly fishing involves using bushy traditional wet fly patterns rather than a delicately designed artificial. Dapping and dry

65

fly also do well with the principal aim being to intercept feeding fish as they travel upwind gobbling emerging mayfly nymphs or spent spinners.

To take a few classic examples, the lochs at Forsinard and at Borgie in central and north Sutherland respectively offer first class mayfly fishing well capable of matching any Irish lough. Local anglers have known this for years and while not exactly keeping it quiet, have largely let the visitor find out for his or her self rather than trumpeting it from the rooftops! The hatch runs from early June to late August if the conditions are right (enough rain to stop the mayfly nymph burrows from drying out) and fishing for the big trout that appear at this time is unsurpassed. It must be remembered that particular times in the day produce profuse hatches and that these core times can vary. Around the warmest part of the day from say 11am to 2pm there is almost always a hatch. Watch for the predictable appearance of gulls swooping low and on to the water. These are sea birds which only come inland to the freshwater lochs during the mayfly bonanza; once it is finished they disappear back to their normal saltwater habitat. A lull in the wind followed by the gulls taking flight from their loch side perches is a sure sign mayfly are hatching.

Sutherland brown trout go through something of a transformation in feeding behaviour during the mayfly hatch. Instead of remaining quiet and out of sight in their normal territories mainly of sheltered food traps, the fish assume more of an active hunting lifestyle swimming up wind lanes or along fertile shorelines to intercept struggling mayflies. For the angler

Sutherland mayfly

Afloat on Modsarie, Borgie, north-west Sutherland

interception is most definitely the key to success; a feeding fish is a taking fish. Traditional flies already mentioned will catch mayfly feeding trout but a really exciting method is to twitch a dry fly like a size 10 French Partridge, Grey Wulff or a similarly sized Golden Olive Bumble made dry with a smear of floatant. Sometimes your fly will be amongst thousands of other hatching insects and will appear to be ignored (it isn't really, it's just the trout have too many choices). In this case it is worthwhile switching to something different. I have found a wet Black Zulu or a Soldier Palmer size 10 to 12 works well when trout are obsessed with surface feeding on natural insects.

Fishing like this on the Forsinard lochs of Slettil or Leir – both shallow waters with a preponderance of marl where the mayfly make their burrows – is dramatically rewarding during mayfly time, equally so the gin-clear weed rich Borgie lochs like Modsarie. Boat or bank fishing is equally productive demanding 100 per cent concentration for the sudden slashing rise of a big trout going for your artificial will often make you jump so much you miss the take completely! Whether you are adrift in the boat or stalking the bank you can often see ascending nymphs floating momentarily on the surface before the struggling insect spreads its wings. At this point the insect is at its most vulnerable and a hefty rise 10 yards away will be followed as quick as a flash by another at 5 yards and another at 1 yard away. Very often this is the same trout on the feed and you must be quick in getting your fly ahead of the fish as they travel at some considerable speed.

Scottish mayfly lochs can compare extremely favourably with the Irish loughs. Scots waters may be a lot smaller but they are no less productive. It is an opportunity many miss in the rush to more and better publicised angling venues waters; ignore Sutherland at your peril...

SECTION 2

ENGLAND

River Test

Chapter 6

FISHING FOR TROUT IN ENGLAND

England's Trout Beginnings

Similar to the rest of the British Isles, the trout of England first became established after colonisation following the last Ice Age some 12,000 years ago. However their survival has followed a much more chequered path than say a largely undisturbed trout population in a remote Scottish lochan, a vast Irish lough or a racing Welsh stream. Pressures from urbanisation and industrialisation over many centuries have seen many original populations of true native English trout diminish in number or change in character even sometimes disappearing altogether. Ten thousand years ago conditions and trout habitat in English lakes and rivers were just as suitable for trout colonisation as in other parts of the UK, it is simply that the burgeoning human population with all its demands sorely depleted the indigenous trout stocks.

It is interesting that the earliest references to the trout of England occur in the eleventh century at which time the fish was called a 'sceote' derived from the Old English term 'sceotan' which means to dart or rush. After the Norman Conquest of 1066 the trout took on its current name probably due to the fact that Norman French named the fish as a 'truht' which in time became corrupted to trout. The next reference to the trout of any consequence comes in the fifteenth century when the *Treatise of Fishing with an Angle* (Dame Juliana Berners) relates that the trout is a 'deyntous fish' i.e. a good source of food and also a 'right feruente byter' meaning an excellent sporting fish worth pursuing with rod and line. There is no doubt that trout were extremely abundant in English rivers and lakes as often fished for by net as they were by rod and line. During Isaac Walton's seventeenth century era, the fish were still basically classed as trout though he did make an attempt to draw attention to the fact that he had observed that there were many kinds of fish 'and of trouts especially, which differ in their bigness, and shape, and spots and colour'.

However in the nineteenth century English theories on the taxonomy of trout underwent a revolution. By then the Swedish scientist Linnaeus circa mid 1700s had already named (Swedish) river trout *Salmo trutta*, sea trout as *Salmo eriox* and brook trout as *Salmo fario* and English scientists readily adopted these classifications. Then in 1836 Englishman William Yarrell added *Salmo ferox* (Lake trout) which he detailed as common to large sheets of water in north England, Scotland and Ireland to the Linnaeus list. Dr Gunther circa 1866 who was principal keeper of the zoological collection of the British Museum, tagged on to this ever growing list his sea trout categories such as Orkney, Galway, East coast and Welsh sea trout and Bull trout common to rivers in the north of England like the Coquet. Gunther also propounded that the trout of Loch Leven in Scotland (*Salmo levenensis*) were another separate species. Now far from simply going trout fishing, anglers of the early to mid nineteenth century were led to believe they were angling for many different species of fish, a prospect which may well have increased their interest in the sport.

Charles Darwin and his theory of evolution (circa 1859) began to halt this splitting of species and later fish biologists followed on Darwin's heels declaring that trout, despite differences in colour and markings, all belonged to the same species *Salmo trutta*. Francis Day writing in 1887 declared in *British and Irish Salmonidae* that as to 'the varieties and hybrids of trout…as seems probable we merely possess one very plastic species subject to an almost unlimited amount of variation…' Day and others followed the Darwinian influence and thus began a reversal of the need to keep separating species; in fact the new thinking scientists became known as 'clumpers' while the old separate species classifiers were known as 'splitters'. Today we simply class English trout along with other northern hemisphere fish as *Salmo trutta* however it is important not to dismiss the ancient English inspired classifications as nonsense. Far from it as they give indications of different genes at work in trout designed to help them survive in particular habitats. The fish may not be different species as such but certainly they can exhibit very different characteristics and this will often determine how we should fish for them. Much work still needs to be done on this fascinating branch of trout science but unfortunately the more pressing environmental issues affecting English trout always seem to get in the way.

Environmental Changes

It is important to understand that unlike the more remote areas of Scotland, parts of Wales and most of Ireland, densely populated England has seen some considerable changes in the quality of its trout habitat and consequent change in the nature of its fish populations. The most critical long term effects on English native trout stocks have come from intensive human, industrial and agricultural practices. These directly led to a change in character if not the complete destruction of the wild trout's environment over several centuries. The density of the English human population, which is significantly greater in number than in Scotland, Ireland and Wales, meant that demands and threats to wild trout have come from many sides. Water has been an essential resource powering industry, providing drinking supplies, assisting agriculture and nurturing animal stock. The need to abstract water from English lakes, reservoirs and rivers for use in the aforementioned has gradually increased sometimes to unsustainable levels and trout have suffered as a consequence. Equally the ingress of industrial waste, effluent, pesticides and sewerage into English watercourses by poorly controlled discharges from factories has been prevalent since very early times and did not come under proper legal control until the early to mid twentieth century. In addition the associated infrastructure of large centres of conurbations such as tarred roads, drainage and sewerage systems can all affect waters normally inhabited by trout. In fact apart from illegal discharges into watercourses, road works are one of the most serious polluters of small streams. Because trout spawn in small offshoots of the main river system their spawning redds are often damaged when redds are situated near to roads. In the rush to make England and parts of central Scotland and south-east Wales the hub of world industry, the humble brown trout has suffered badly.

Effective laws against pollution of English watercourses did not really come into play until the first half of the twentieth century and even then these have proved hard to enforce and unfortunately by then significant damage had already been done. The Salmon and Freshwater Fishery Act of 1923 declared that 'no person shall cause or knowingly permit to flow, or put or knowingly permit to put into any waters containing fish or into any tributaries thereof, any liquid or solid matter to such an extent as to cause the waters to be poisonous or injurious to fish or the spawning grounds, spawn or food of fish and if any person contravenes this section he shall be guilty of an offence against this Act.' Further environmental protection bodies with

In England much natural spawning habitat has been lost

statutory powers came into being during the twentieth century including the National Rivers Authority, Her Majesty's Inspectorate of Pollution and various local authorities' waste regulators. The Environment Agency (EA) was formed in 1995 and this brought together all the aforementioned groups under one umbrella. The EA has statutory responsibility in England and Wales for pollution prevention and control, flood defence, water resources, fisheries, conservation, navigation and water based recreation. Sadly by the time it was formed most of the severe harm to trout stocks had already occurred nevertheless the EA has given important legal back up to the preservation of trout, something which Scotland with its splintered approach of Civil Law and Protection Orders has still yet to achieve.

Restocking

As in Scotland, escalating demand for fishing coupled with environmental deterioration of natural waterways meant that restocking became the first choice as a quick fix for England's apparently depleting trout stocks. From the latter half of the nineteenth century and right through the twentieth century sport fisheries flourished particularly in domestic reservoirs built to cope with increased public demand for water near to the main centres of conurbation. Fly fishing generally became hugely popular whether on still or flowing water and as anglers past and present generally measured their success in the numbers of fish in the bag, the fishers demanded ever bigger supplies of trout be placed in their favourite waters. The assumption was that more trout automatically meant more chance of action. Right from the word go scant regard was paid to the genetic changes brought about by introducing brown trout with differing characteristics to the native species. Neither was much thought given to the idea that the wild indigenous trout could actually sustain themselves by natural reproduction if both fishing and environmental practices near watercourses were better controlled. Past popular thinking especially in the Victorian era promoted 'new blood' as an important asset in a healthy trout population. By throwing more and more fish into a fishery it was thought it would immediately improve. We now know this is not the case and that intensive restocking practice can alter the nature of a fishery not always to its betterment however in the past a holistic view was a rare find.

Though the art of pisciculture i.e. the rearing of fish by artificial means, has been around since the days of the ancient Chinese Dynasties and the Roman Empire it seems only to have arrived in force in England after the 1850s. In Europe various fish culture experiments conducted in Germany and France in the eighteenth and mid nineteenth centuries had shown it possible to successfully rear freshwater trout from the egg stage. In 1854 a Piscicultural Institution was established in Alsace where a Monsieur Coste devised the first system of rearing trout eggs on glass rods kept fresh with clean flowing water. This method was quickly taken up by both English and Scottish fish culturists and the system was used right up until the 1960s when zinc and then stainless steel replaced the glass grilles.

The skills of the fish culturalists might have been adroit but their understanding of the effects of continually adding new stock into indigenous fish populations left much to be desired. There was money to be made in supplying flourishing local fishings with vast quantities of 'stockies' and few passed by this opportunity in the name of sustainable ecology. Unfortunately as with so many other things in UK fishing, a considerable degree of dogma and controversy quickly built up around the apparent need to restock waters. On the one hand there were a number of prominent English scientists like Frank Buckland and Sir James Maitland both circa 1880s who stoutly promoted trout stocking as the only way of 'improving' a fishery and on the other we have no less a luminary than F M Halford claiming that natural reproduction alone in a river is often sufficient to keep up the stock. At the time Halford received little in the way of praise for taking this more moderate and sensible view in fact he was roundly ridiculed by Colonel Custance in the late nineteenth century book *The Trout*, written by the Marquess of Granby. Custance sniped at Halford's ideas saying that they were 'an exploded theory' and that restocking was always justified as it was born out by the 'careful statistics of figures'. We all know now about lies, damned lies and statistics and over a hundred years on it is perhaps no coincidence that it is Halford we remember, Custance being long forgotten. It seems that just as Scotland had its divisions of angling thought, so did its larger neighbour!

Misguided if well intentioned thinking on stock additions apart, the English fish biologists of one hundred and fifty years ago must be acknowledged as being remarkably adept in not only raising good quality trout but also exporting them to far flung places around the globe. In 1862 Frank Buckland requested that fifteen hundred trout eggs be included in a shipment of salmon eggs to Australia and New Zealand. After three months being cared for at sea in the sailing ship the *Beautiful Star*, approximately three hundred trout eggs survived and went on to be planted out in the Plenty River in Tasmania. From 1868 the Plenty River became the natural breeding ground for the imported British trout and these fish were used as a source of eggs and fry for Australia, New Zealand and rivers in Tasmania. After this success, British trout introductions continued apace across the globe with fish successfully planted out in India, South Africa, Newfoundland, Argentina and Chile.

American Rainbow Trout

The first consignment of American rainbow trout eggs arrived in England in 1884 and after a little hesitation over the imported fish's strong migratory tendencies which impelled them to leave a stillwater by any route including drainage ditches and inlet pipes, both the English angler and the fish culturalists embraced the nouveau trout with the greatest of fervour. There were several reasons for this and whether the modern thinking angler approves or not, the 'rainbow rationale' has prevailed in England for well over a hundred years.

So what is this rationale? First and foremost the rainbow has proved a big hit with anglers for so long because it was usually somewhat easier to catch than the wild brown. This is especially so if it had been reared in stew ponds for a year or two before being released. 'Hand' feeding practices have ensured that the rainbow trout, far from fleeing from a shadow on the shore, has quickly became human orientated. The fish have in effect been conditioned to the fact that the potential predator i.e. the man on the bank, was not going to harm them but will actually supply them with an easily accessible source of food! Brown trout on the other hand have never had such a developed tendency to 'follow the feeder' and have remained the far more cautious of the two species. This apparent tameness (anglers then and now call it 'boldness' in taking the fly which is not strictly true) has ensured that the rainbow has been the first choice for stocking fisheries where anglers have demanded almost guaranteed bag limits in return for their money.

Another critical factor in choosing to stock rainbows is the fast growth rate inherent in this trout. Why on earth should fish culturalists wait several years for an English brown trout to grow and put on enough weight for an angler to want to catch him when the faster growing rainbow could supply a takeable fish in half the time? By weighting his stock policies toward rainbows rather than browns the fish farmer could ensure that he had a much higher turnover of fish to add to his pond/lake and in doing so increased his income quite substantially. Rainbows too were said to offer considerably more sport than solitary browns as they were

Today in England the fast growing rainbow is often the first choice to stock

given to acrobatic tendencies and fought well. Also the fish obligingly swam around the stock pond in a shoal and anglers would know that having hooked one they could if quick make contact with several more by standing in the one spot on the shore. Anglers after the brown trout had and still have to move along the bank and cover new fish territories, thus the rainbow saved quite a bit of time spent walking for the angler on the shore.

Given that the faster growing freer-rising rainbow seemed to be the answer to both the angler and fish-growers' prayers, little wonder England was to see huge introductions of the American interloper from the 1880s onward. There were detractors to the rainbow cause but they did not come until at least thirty years after the first new stock arrived. Ernest Philips notably denounced rainbows in his book *Trout in Lakes and Reservoirs*. Philips said that rainbows were of 'no use at all in rivers' as they quickly disappeared owing to their ingrained migratory tendencies. Nothing new in that as such but he then states that for stillwater stocking, rainbows were in his opinion, only of limited use especially where a water was to be only periodically stocked with both rainbow and brown. He observed that on some small mixed fish waters the introduced rainbows would feed avidly and be captured in their first year of introduction, in the second year they were caught in roughly the same number as the resident brown but in the third year only browns were captured as the rainbows all but disappeared. This meant the fishery had to be annually stocked with rainbows otherwise anglers desiring these particular fish would go elsewhere. Philips also claimed that rainbows were prone to sulking on the bottom if not completely disappearing altogether from stillwaters. J C Mottram in 1924 also declared in his book *Trout Fisheries – their Care and Preservation* that rainbows were exceptionally greedy fish and 'if put in suitable water ate up much (brown) trout food to no purpose'. Neither did he think they were of much use in cold shallow water adding that he thought 'lakes where there is deep water 12 to 20ft, to which they (the rainbows) retire for warmth during the winter' were much better habitat for rainbows.

Both Philips' and Mottram's opinions hold as much water today and they did in the early twentieth century but both have been largely ignored and rainbow stocking has continued regardless. Few scientists have been prepared to stand up and be counted on the apparent necessity of stocking rainbows sometimes of dubious quality and in overblown quantities. Indeed it was not until the 1990s that the eminent fisheries scientists Maitland and Campbell called into question some British rainbow stocking practices. In their book *Freshwater Fishes* they discussed the stocking of very large 'trophy' fish for anglers to catch stating that 'a high proportion of the large rainbow trout used for stocking are elderly retired broodstock and the objective seems to be to put them into a fishery and then angle for them before they die of old age or starvation'. Today trophy trout can be grown on by a combination of over feeding and in some cases genetic manipulation, neither practice being at all natural. Maitland and Campbell also alluded to stunted poor quality rainbows being found in small waters which had been relentlessly overstocked. Their findings helped to confirm the fact that over exploitation of the rainbow had been prevalent in England and other parts of the UK for many years and that the results were not always positive.

Fortunately the general tide of angling opinion now seems to have turned a corner with fishers usually keener to enjoy less intensively stocked waters with better quality fish. While it can be considered the rainbow trout serves an important purpose in taking pressure off wild stocks it must also be remembered that a specimen with ragged fins, dark slimy coat and broken tail bears absolutely no resemblance to the dashing silver purple flashed thick set rainbow which left its native streams of the Pacific coast of North America in the 1880s. In fact such poor quality trout bred in the UK are an insult to what is undoubtedly a supreme USA native fish. Choose your venue with care and support those who promote good fish practice.

Twenty-first Century English Trout

It is now a hard fact that the bulk of trout anglers in England fish for the stocked non-native rainbow rather than the indigenous brown trout. While Scotland, Ireland and specific rivers in Wales still sustain healthy and relatively profuse stocks of naturally reproducing wild trout, England has struggled to match its neighbouring countries' abundance of fish. Even where an exclusively brown trout fishery exists it is often supplemented by introduced stock rather than relying on purely native naturally spawned fish. There are a few relatively unchanged

fishing venues still in existence but these are well in the minority. One important point to consider is that despite its abundance, the rainbow trout does not normally breed naturally in English waters. A 1971 survey of rainbow trout in the UK showed only three sites in the south of England which had self sustained rainbow trout spawning. More of a nuisance is the number of escapees from trout farms which enter river systems without being officially stocked. These rainbows are roving and competitive feeders and often displace any resident browns as they work their greedy way through a river system. This means an accidental fish escape several miles upstream can quickly sweep its way along the entire river course and disturb the ecology of the stream.

For all that, the overall picture for trout fishing in England is an interesting one with considerable opportunities to fish for rainbows in some outstandingly beautiful pastoral settings close to, yet remote from, town and industry and also to try for brownies on a few select rivers in the northern reaches and southern corners of this green and pleasant land.

Chapter 7

TROUT TACTICS IN ENGLAND

First Methods of English Trout Fishing

Just as in Scotland the earliest methods of English trout fishing before rod and line were by netting, hand lines or catching fish in traps. Trout and salmon would be harvested in this way to provide a much needed source of food. Perhaps of more interest are the very early angling efforts made purely with hook and line. When employing multiple hooks this method was known as long lining. A length of line with a large number of hooks attached would be strung out from stakes on the shore or would be 'fished' from the end of a boat. This method would be used mainly in salt water but there would obviously be opportunities for it to be employed in fresh water especially on or near river mouths where migratory salmon and sea trout could be easily intercepted. In Scotland a similar fishing tactic was used with otter boarding which was to all intents and purposes the same as long lining only it employed a wooden float system.

Barbed fishing hooks made of iron have been found dating back to the Anglo Saxon times (tenth century AD) and it is thought the angling lines of that era would have been made of nettle hemp. The nettle was and still is a common weed plant in the UK. It is thought that to make a 'yarn' the stems were first immersed in water for several hours, then pulped so that individual fibre strands would be obtained. These fibres would then be spun like wool into a tough yarn which was then used in the making of nets, fishing line and archers' bow strings. Fish were also caught by hand lining, a technique which used the same materials but on a single hook basis with a bored stone weight attached on the line's end to make the baited hook sink to the required depth. Early fishing nets were also made of nettle hemp and these were principally strung across rivers in order to catch migratory salmon and trout though some historians believe they may also have been used to section off particular areas of the river perhaps for fish breeding purposes. Fish traps made of wicker were also used in flowing rivers and estuaries to trap running fish and eels. Whatever ancient method was used it was mainly done to enrich the human food supply rather than for sport.

Early Rod and Line in England

It would seem that the English rod and line method of trout fishing first became popular not long after the Norman invasion of 1066 and though there is no way of proving it, the first rod and line used for trout in England may well have been wielded by an invader from Europe rather than an Englishman. Though it is all a bit academic now, in the past the European influence was particularly strong especially from France where trout angling was practised from the twelfth century if not earlier. The first really serious attempt to chronicle European and English skills in fly fishing for trout came in the world famous book *Treatise of Fishing with an Angle* compiled in 1496 by Dame Juliana Berners. This milestone tome brings together historical fishing knowledge from perhaps a hundred years earlier and draws heavily on other books of the period notably from France. Although Dame Juliana is often credited as

the author it is likely she acted in part more as an editor bringing together other works and then commented on them rather than writing the entire book herself. Nevertheless the information recorded gives a thorough insight into the remarkably well developed angling skills of fifteenth century England.

It is worthwhile briefly reiterating a few details from the *Treatise* as over five hundred years later some of the general skills mentioned are still in common use. In that era the equipment was basic but serviceable. Rods were of two pieces, long and pliable, lines were strands of horse hair, hooks were iron and usually fashioned from tailors' or embroiderers' needles. Reels are not mentioned as these appeared later in sporadic use in the late 1600s and did not come into common use until the early nineteenth century. Flies were of simple construction, the *Treatise* lists twelve, many of which are still in use in adapted forms today. These flies were to be made as definite imitations of insects rather than vague general patterns. We know the *Treatise* flies were amongst others, the stone fly, mayfly, alder fly, yellow dun and olive dun. The *Treatise* states that these patterns were to be used at specific times of the year to imitate hatches of seasonally occurring insects. If you have always assumed 'matching the hatch' to be a relatively new concept, think again for it was commonly in use in 1496 thus confirming the fact that there is nothing new in fishing!

The *Treatise* also makes astute comments on what we now call watercraft with discussion on the effect of changing weather conditions, the best time to fish, the necessity to spoon trout to see what they were feeding on and the best places to try for trout. Advice which must have been common knowledge in this early era was also given on striking and playing a trout however it is interesting that absolutely no instruction is given about physically casting a fly. As the horsehair line was simply attached to the end of the rod it is likely that a wind-assisted dap was the most probable option but the skill of presenting a fly by a definite cast was not really described for another one hundred and twenty years or so when a William Lawson first mentions learning 'the cast of the fly' in correspondence published in 1620. Even if the *Treatise* may have seen some plagiarism from other sources it contained wonderfully succinct descriptions not least that you go fishing 'for your solace, to procure the health of your body and especially of your soul'.

Progress in English fishing seems slow in the immediate years that followed the *Treatise*, Mascall wrote *A Book of Fishing with Hook and Line* in 1590 but apart from his theories on fish culture which were quite advanced for the time Mascall did not appear to make any giant leaps forward in terms of wielding rod and line. He did record the use of double hooks (wee doubles in Scotland) thought to be a Celtic invention, but now it seems from southern climes. In addition he mentions making flies with a cork body in order to make them float – a precursor to the dry fly perhaps? However it was not until the mid to late 1600s that English angling went through another era of change and development. This is the time of important pioneers such as Venables, Walton and Cotton, names to be conjured with, all very different in their styles of writing yet all obviously knowledgeable fishers.

Sir Isaac Walton's milestone work *The Compleat Angler* was first published in 1653 and though it borrows in part from the *Treatise* this book served the purpose of bringing English fly fishing skills together and updating them. Cotton was to write the *Compleat Angler* Part 2 in 1676 and being a close friend of Walton wrote in very similar vein and made sure established traditions were upheld regarding the use of fly rod and line in imitative fly fishing. Cotton was a proponent of 'fishing at the top' and in this sense fished flies as they fell on or near the water surface i.e. dry or almost dry. Venables is perhaps the lesser known of the trio yet he was a considerable innovator being the first to write with clarity on the techniques of using upstream or downstream (wet) fly. He was the first to make a distinction between how a fly could be cast and discusses the merits of each technique and from this it would seem that upstream wet fly was relatively well established prior to Scotland's W C Stewart expounding its virtues in the 1800s. Venables, along with Cotton and Walton must also be credited as pioneering exponents of casting to a rising trout rather than just fishing the water in a random way.

Between the 1600s and 1800s English angling made slow but steady progress moving from long rods, no reels, twisted hair lines and single flies to shorter rods complete with reel, silk fly lines and leaders of gut to which either a single or a little team of wet flies would be attached. It would appear that regarding the use of multiple flies there may have been a cross border transference from Scotland to England of this skill. Unfortunately who copied who is lost in the mists of antiquity which, given the two nations' past warring history might be just as well! The next earth shattering angling advance did not happen until the late 1800s but when it did it took the trout angling scene by storm. Esteemed angler F M Halford began to strongly promote the use of the single dry fly. Though a number of other anglers had mentioned dry or floating flies in their writings notably Stoddart, Pulman, Francis, Scotcher, Mascall and Marryat it is the ground breaking works of Halford that cemented dry fly into the annals of English fly fishing. Though we will look in more detail at Halford in the section *Fishing the Dry Fly*, it is safe to say there is no one more influential in this branch of English trout fishing. To strike a balance we will also look at the perfect foil to Halford and his followers, the esteemed G M Skues who answered the burgeoning cult of dry fly with some well thought nymph tactics.

No brief summary of the roots of English trout fishing is complete without reference to the lesser publicised but no less skilled branch of angling developed in the 'north country'. This technique centres on wet fly fishing on northern English rivers in Yorkshire, Lancashire, Northumberland and Cumbria. The skills required here developed separately from those on the southern chalkstreams and often required fishing downstream with sparse wet flies. Amongst the main nineteenth century promoters of north country techniques were Theakston, Jackson and Pritt who all wrote expertly on the flies and skills for use in the rushing streams of northern England. Unfortunately their concepts were almost completely overshadowed by the cultish promotion of the upstream dry fly happening almost simultaneously in the south of England. While the old north country skills have not been lost and will be further discussed in this book, it is important to remember the need to follow fishing fashion was a powerful influence in England and that this sometimes caused other equally important skills to receive less attention.

But before we progress into the range of English tactics let's look for a moment at dapping for though this skill is never commonly associated with England there are some interesting references which cannot be ignored...

Dapping on English Waters

The art of dapping normally conjures up images of big rods and wafting floss lines afloat on Irish or Scottish lochans and it might come as some surprise to learn that a reasonable amount of evidence exists that English fly fishing also has ancient roots in this branch of the sport. The fact that the Europeans imported hugely long rods into England sometimes known as Bolognese rods and that early attempts at 'casting' a fly with these would be a wind assisted affair, means that a form of dapping was the likely first fly fishing expertise in common use in England. Walton in the mid seventeenth century mentions dapping or using the 'dop' moving

According to nineteenth century writing dapping was at one time employed on the Test

the fly as if it were alive with a short line and natural insects like the grasshopper or the hawthorn fly. This was really more akin to a form of surreptitious bait fishing – in fact Walton also recommends hiding behind a tree to execute the dap!

While it can be assumed that prior to the invention of reels to store lines, all English fly fishing techniques like those of the rest of the UK amounted to a form of dapping, there are some very interesting specific references to English dapping on the River Test of all hallowed places! Writing in the late 1880s Colonel Custance in *The Trout* refers to information given to him by W G Craven a member of the Longstock Club on the Test. Craven refers to fishing mayflies specifically on this river and states 'Til about 1868 the only flies used were large ones, mayflies and moths being the most common artificial ones. Early in the century the "blow line" was introduced from Ireland, the natural fly on a No 8 hook being used. For this purpose a hollow cane rod of some 24ft was the general weapon.' He then adds that in his time (1890s approx) 'such a proceeding is hardly ever heard of in English rivers.' Craven's statement implies that the skill of dapping had not necessarily been carried down from Walton's days in the 1600s and instead had been re-introduced via Ireland at the beginning of the nineteenth century. Whichever is true we will never know. However, to find the ancient art of dapping has been practised at all on the Test would have driven the long succession of 'dry fly' purists that followed apoplectic had they known!

83

While dapping skills have continued in use on larger Irish and Scottish waters where it would be seen as a form of 'traditional' angling sitting comfortably beside the wet fly, dapping has largely fallen into disuse on English waters mainly due to advances in tackle design and the far reaching social pressures linked to dry fly fishing. It could perhaps be said that the English angler is more easily led in angling fashion or conversely that he is more willing to advance into new skills than his compatriots across the rest of the UK, but we will let you make your own mind on that...

Chapter 8

SKILLS FOR ENGLISH RIVERS

Wet Fly on the River

As we have already seen with the discussion on early rod and line techniques there seems to be general agreement that the first type of fly angling in England would be with flies fished as they fell. In other words if the fly landed and floated on the surface it was fished 'dry' on the current, whereas when the fly's feathers became heavy and wet it would sink and would be fished largely as a 'sunk' fly. It is important to remember that prior to the defining dry fly revolution in the nineteenth century there was no absolute distinction made between wet fly and dry, in fact there appears to be no reference as to who first attached the title 'wet' to his or her fly. Also to be considered is the fact that the first wet flies were almost always made with a wing, a palmered hackle or a wing and head hackle, flies made like nymphs did not seem to feature.

Another important point to bear in mind is that England, especially southern England, is never really thought of as the first home of traditional wet fly fishing; Scotland, Ireland or indeed Wales might lay claim to this title but England is more distanced from it. This is perhaps because the earliest pioneers of English trout fishing often described their fishing techniques as 'fishing at the top' which means the fly was fished on or very near the water surface. Cotton first described it thus in the 1670s and was obviously recording already well established practices. Quite simply the long rods and light horsehair line of old which fished 'fine and far off' did not allow the fly to sink much anyway. This is not to say the usefulness of the sunk fly was not recognised; James Chetham in his *Anglers' Vade Mecum* 1681 tellingly wrote that 'All fish take the fly sometimes best at the top of the water, at another time much better a little under. Therefore if they will not rise at the top, try a little under'. Note Chetham's order of recounting these early fishing tactics. He used a semi-floating fly first throw followed by a sunk wet if it didn't produce the goods, not the other way around. He is also purported to have described wet fly dressings with soft hackles which would be the first step in making the fly sink quicker. Soft hackle flies then went on to be the trademark of traditional wet fly river fishing. Unfortunately Chetham's simple yet highly practical advice was largely forgotten at least in the south of England when the dry fly epoch came in and the old wet fly river skills were pushed aside as *passé* and outdated.

In the latter 1800s it was left to some largely unsung heroes mainly but not exclusively from the northern counties, to keep the art of English wet fly going. Pioneers such as Swarbrick, Bainbridge, Ronalds, Jackson and Pritt are now largely forgotten however each played a part in recorded and developing important sunk wet fly tactics from the north of the country. Ronalds circa 1836 was particularly influential as he was the first angling author to systematically relate artificial flies to natural insects and record them all complete with illustrations and dressings. For many years this catalogue of naturals and imitations was the standard work for fly tyers as it overcame the difficulties of deciding what insect an old traditional pattern was meant to represent. Most of Ronalds' patterns featured a down wing and although he intended to have them used as floating flies fishing them on or near the water surface like his predecessors, they actually went on to form the mainstay of English wet fly imitative patterns. Unfortunately this ground breaking list had one fundamental error in that Ronalds, despite painstakingly observing what trout fed on at his local river, omitted to mention specific nymph patterns to represent trout food emanating from the river bottom rather than falling on it from above. It is doubtful that this was deliberate, the preceding four hundred years of English fishing history had already decried that flies were to be fished as imitations 'at the top' and Ronalds would find such historic doctrine a considerable obstacle to bypass.

North Country Wet Fly Fishing

Through the latter half of the nineteenth century and into the twentieth century there was a gradual but sustained separation of common river fishing techniques across England, the northern reaches continued to favour wet fly while the south thoroughly embraced the dry fly. While fashion has a part to play in this, the main reason for this skills division is actually a sound ecological one. Northern streams have a roughness and rapidity to them not found in the altogether balmier chalkstreams of the southern quarter. The fast flowing water means that most northern trout are used to taking their insect food in a submerged or partially submerged state. It therefore goes without saying that techniques need to be different.

One of the tomes on northern England wet fly river fishing most referred to is the book by Edmonds and Lee *Brook and River Trouting* published in 1916. This amalgamated nineteenth century river wet fly skills in highly practical fashion with the authors advocating upstream or downstream wet fly, or worm or dry fly to be used according to the conditions. Their recommended fly patterns are sparse delicate affairs and are usually tied Spider fashion akin in name to Scotland's W C Stewart's flies; these have now become universally known as 'North Country Trout Flies'. It is also interesting that the wet flies of northern England were fished in teams just as in Scotland indicating a largely un-referred to amount of cross border transferral of skills. Fishing for them with wet fly can be done either up or downstream however Edmonds and Lee emphasise that the art of fishing downstream on an English river bears no relation whatsoever to the Scottish 'across and down' method. Downstream wet fly according to Edmonds and Lee meant casting slightly up and across and then letting the flies drift naturally down in the current without drag while the angler works his way slowly down the river bank, in other words it is the angler who goes downstream not the flies. This tactic was apparently of particular use when the river was high and/or coloured and the fish were not rising freely.

Fishing wet fly upstream was and still is the most used tactic on northern trout rivers not necessarily casting at rising fish but rather the fly is targeted at likely trout holding spots such as the slack water behind boulders, eddies and channels were food has collected and trout will be lying. The flies are cast on a short line and then worked with raised rod tip with rapid casting required to explore each nook and cranny without the line and fly dragging. There is a real art to judging both the quality of trout habitat to explore and the repetitive casting of a delicate upstream wet fly, so much so it can safely be said that this style of north country fishing is not really for the inexperienced angler. Perhaps this is why it has never achieved the popularity of other forms of English river angling though it is still highly prevalent in certain areas.

North Country Soft Hackle Flies

The signature flies of the north country are fast sinking soft hackle wet patterns. They are imitative flies designed to imitate a sub surface insect either in nymph or emerging stage

A typical selection of wet flies in use today

being washed down in the current. The flies first appeared in common use during the 1800s though they may actually be a lot older and they are still in regular use today. Patterns range from the famous Partridge and Orange, Waterhen Bloa and Snipe and Purple through to less well known patterns like the Dark Watchet or the Light Needle. Like Scotland's Tummel Flies and Stewart's Spiders the dressings for these flies were extremely sparse and delicate and required some dexterity in their construction. As previously described they are normally fished upstream.

The secrets of the soft hackle flies' success lies in two important factors. First they have a sparseness which allows the fly to sink quickly in fast currents and second the soft hackle pulses with a kick quite naturally in the water just like a small struggling insect. Because the flies were used in close proximity to the Scottish English border it was and still is common practice for one country to claim they first invented these flies but that's history for you. The truth is soft hackle flies have stood the test of time admirably and are still in common use across the UK today.

Stonefly and Creeper Fishing

It is important to realise that the northern rivers of England have never enjoyed the prolific mayfly hatches of the southern chalkstreams. However they do have good stonefly (*Perlidae*) numbers and the prevalence of this big mouthful of an insect has led anglers to fish them as bait in the nymph creeper stage. The creeper is extracted from the river bed and then put on a small hook and cast upstream working it back on a raised rod tip. In Scotland this was and still is referred to as gadger fishing and is often used on rivers like the Clyde. North country fishers have also used the natural insect impaled on small hooks fished in similar fashion to the Scots, calling it creeper fishing. Flies to imitate the prolific stonefly hatch include the Winter Brown and the Dark Needle and these flies are of ancient origin indicating that the stonefly has long been recognised as an important part of the north country angler's armoury. Stoneflies were and occasionally still are referred to as the mayflies of the north which can confuse visiting anglers no end especially American ones who refer to all their Ephemera as mayflies!

The Dry Fly Revolution

While soft hackle flies and upstream wets have long been associated with fishing tactics for the rivers of northern England it can be said that the dry fly was essentially born and bred on the southern chalkstreams. Compared to the many centuries of wet fly angling, or at least flies which fished 'at the top', the dry fly is a comparative newcomer to English rivers. Flies dressed to float did not appear in common use until the early to mid 1800s and even then they were mainly to be found in use on the streams of southern England. Who first invented dries is now academic, fly tyer James Ogden in the early nineteenth century claimed to be the originator but then there had been others referring to using dry or floating flies before him. Ogden was also one of the first to describe casting a dry fly ahead of a rising fish and letting it drift down without 'a ripple' a term which quickly became associated with the dreaded fish scaring 'drag'. In addition English angler Cholmondeley Pennell wrote a now largely forgotten book *Fishing with the Dry Fly* in 1870 and this gave considerable detail on not only how to fish a dry fly but also how to construct it. He made no claim to inventing the dry fly but describes a number of fly designs already in existence. These dry flies he stated were made with paired upright wings tied in so that the feathers sat upright with convex surfaces. Interestingly this fly tying technique was the same as that detailed by Halford et al some sixteen years later so it would appear that both Pennell and Halford recorded already established fly tying techniques.

Even though the mystery of the exact originator of the dry fly will never be solved amongst those earlier dry fly exponents, today it is the name of F M Halford we instantly recall when discussing the dry fly. He wrote his epoch-making books *Floating Flies and how to Dress Them* (1886) followed by *Dry Fly Fishing in Theory and Practice* (1891) and from these tomes the art of making and using dry flies became firmly established. Halford's theories fitted in ably with the fashions of the Victorian period and in next to no time the cult of the dry fly swept first across southern England and then further afield. It is interesting that while it is Halford we recognise as the principal promoter of dry fly, his friend the shy, retiring George Selwyn Marryat was also of considerable assistance to the cause.

The dry version of the March Brown is typical of the fashion of turning good wet flies into dry ones

Indeed Halford is thought to have got a good many of his ideas on fly design directly from Marryat (see River Frome page 113). Halford and Marryat were the technicians of dry fly making, both were concerned at the lack of uniformity of dry flies sold in shops during the 1880s and methodically set about standardising methods of fly tying. Despite the fact Halford gained much of his knowledge in dry fly design from Marryat, the latter did not put his name as a co-author of Halford's book on floating flies, preferring to remain out of the limelight. Thus Halford's trademark flies tied with paired upright wings quite probably came from the flies being made by Marryat who himself may have adapted them from earlier tyings.

Halford's dry flies belong to the school of exact imitation and in this he was painstakingly precise, for example his mayfly patterns were copied exactly from the colours he observed in the natural insect. He also was the first to produce a series of dry flies roughly in the size of the insect they were meant to imitate. Prior to Halford doing this, most dries were tied as imitations of large insects i.e. mayfly and were therefore rather cumbersome to cast. All credit to FMH for producing not only imitations of mayfly but also smaller olives, black gnats, sedges and brown ants. These flies were all tied with a fairly dense head hackle and long balancing tail which helped the fly's buoyancy considerably. Halford's correct matching of the hatch was quickly taken up by the fly tying fashionistas of the nineteenth and early twentieth centuries with the result that many ancient wet fly patterns were suddenly turned into dry flies with 'cocked' i.e. bold upright wings. In some cases this worked well but in others wet fly traditions which had been effective for hundreds of years were lost in a veritable tidal wave of floating patterns.

Fishing the Dry Fly

Just as the exact originator of the first dry fly is undecided, who devised the technique of how a dry fly should be fished is open to question. Attempts were obviously being made in the

1850s to fish dry fly, an article by the 'Hampshire Fly Fisher' stated that fishing upstream was very awkward 'unless you are trying the Carshalton dodge and fishing dry fly'. Carshalton was on the River Wandle and the 'Carshalton dodge' appears to have been an angler's false cast which in the days prior to chemical floatants would potentially aid the drying of the feathers of the fly and make it float better. Across Britain between 1850 and 1870 further references to dry fly begin to appear. Scottish angler Thomas Stoddart mentions false casting to dry the fly in the 1850s so there was obviously some thought going into how to fish the floating fly effectively. In 1857 Francis wrote of fishing upstream with a dry fly and letting it drift back down over the trout in a natural way. Ten years later he was to write that the use of dry fly had become 'systemic' in the south of England especially on the chalkstreams. In addition the cause was also greatly helped in the 1880s by the discovery that the application of paraffin to the feathers of the fly helped it to float better and later by the development of the first silk floating lines.

At whatever time you look at English dry fly river fishing it seems the key to its success has always hinged on casting upstream ahead of a rising trout using an imitation of a hatched surface insect while keeping yourself out of view of the trout. In the late nineteenth century Halford and his vociferous followers, of which he had many, decreed a set of conditions which were to be vigourously followed, not to do so being considered highly unsporting not to say ungentlemanly. These rules centred not only on casting upstream of a rising trout with a good imitation of the natural winged insect but also that the dry fly used should be of the correct size and colour and that it should float down to the waiting trout on the water surface in a 'cocked' position without drag. This pedantic technique became forever known as 'purist'.

90 | *The author fishing a modern upstream dry*

Unfortunately some of Halford's later followers developed this technique to such an extent that they became obsessed with only casting to a rising fish and not fishing at all if no trout were seen to be feeding! This frankly silly behaviour was in keeping with the social snobberies of the period and it became known as 'ultra purist'. It is interesting that even Halford himself thought such a high degree of selective but inflexible angling was unnecessary. In the late nineteenth century he actually wrote 'Although respecting their (the ultra purists) scruples this is in my humble opinion riding the hobby (of upstream dry) to death'. In addition he also defended across and down tactics albeit with a dry fly rather than a traditional wet in certain difficult circumstances like high winds or casting obstructions.

By the beginnings of the First World War in 1914 Halford, perhaps spurred on by his fanatical followers, let go of any of his more liberalist views and assumed the mantle of dry fly upstream only on his hallowed chalkstreams. As he grew into old age his views became that much more entrenched and even when they were patently wrong as in the case of the effectiveness of the upstream nymph purported by Skues (see below), Halford stuck rigidly to his guns. This was a pity for other notable anglers of the period were also appealing for a greater degree of flexibility in fishing tactics. Sir Edward Grey in his worthy tome *Fly Fishing* (1900) discusses the merits of dry fly and wet and concludes 'It is not necessary, nor even appropriate, to exalt the one at the expense of the other'. Yet despite the dogma and doctrine Halford must be remembered as the bringer of dry fly to the angling masses albeit by a rather fanatical route first in southern England and then right across the whole of the UK. All fishing would be the poorer without his vital contributions.

The Nymph on the River

It is odd that southern England exponents of the dry fly apparently took an inordinate time to recognise the fact that trout feed below the water surface just as much as they take insects off the top. Some chalkstream diehards of the Halford era refused point blank to recognise that ancient wet fly patterns were designed to imitate natural sub surface food and instead purported wet flies to be inferior general attractor patterns. Looking back at the late nineteenth and early twentieth centuries there was a definite split in fishing and fly tying methods between the north of England and the south. In northern England the sparse soft hackle wet flies, first constructed to represent submerged insects either as nymphs or emergers, were in uninterrupted use from around 1800 while in the south anglers first stuck rigidly to winged wet flies until Halford and his dry fly design arrived after which many anglers rushed to embrace the dry and forgot about using the wet fly altogether.

Fortunately in the late 1800s certain anglers began to seriously question the new unwritten laws regarding angling on the southern chalkstreams. Why did no one recognise the fact that trout feed sub surface? Why was the angler being forced to always use an upstream dry fly no matter the conditions and why could he only cast a particular fly to obviously feeding fish? Why were there rules being introduced forcing the angler to fish upstream dry on the chalkstreams even when it was patently obvious it would not work? Spending an inordinate amount of time waiting to see a visibly rising trout so as to begin angling seemed to some to be an inordinate waste of good fishing time.

And who was it who dared to ask these searching questions especially with Halford and his followers so loudly on purist song? Step forward the balancing foil of Mr G M Skues who wrote a series of books astutely propounding the use of the upstream nymph and in doing so mightily annoyed the chalkstream purists! The patterns designed by Skues worked. They caught trout where others failed, so much so that Halford was forced to make some sort of

91

reply to the success rate of the nymph. Defensibly he said 'the difficulty does not lie in dressing an artificial grub representing the dun nymph, but imparting to that imitation the motion and direction taken by the natural insect at that stage of its existence'. In other words Halford made out that fishing an upstream nymph effectively was not possible. This was at the most complete nonsense or to say the least, a limp excuse. By taking such a defensive stance all he did was confirm a narrow but not unexpected prejudice against anything which might match the effectiveness of the dry fly particularly on his beloved chalkstreams.

Skues on Fishing the Upstream Nymph

It is said that in the late 1890s pioneering angler G M Skues came upon the nymph by happy accident having found a rather useless dry fly pattern which sank abysmally actually caught more trout than a standard floating dry when cast upstream of a rising trout. Skues fished the chalkstreams of the Itchen and the Kennet just as Halford did and can be credited with just as much innovative skill. However while Halford concentrated his efforts on designing the perfect dry, one which floated like a dream with its hackles forever cocked, Skues concerned himself much more with the nuts and bolts of fish behaviour and how to overcome difficult angling situations. Skues observed that a bulging rise was a trout actively feeding on nymphs sub surface and therefore it was a fish which could be caught. Up until Skues' studies, many of the dry fly men had assumed such an 'underwater' rise was simply a trout getting ready to make a move on a surface insect about to hatch.

Skues also recorded that trout took an artificial for reasons of hunger, caprice, curiosity or tyranny and that quite often these feeding modes occurred sub surface rather than solely when taking food coming from above in an obvious hatch. In addition he propounded the theory that the nymphing trout had to be struck into rather than simply hooked when it was visibly taking insects on the water surface. This he said could be done by watching and anticipating a 'little brown wink' under the water which would be the signal that the trout had turned on the fly. All these innovative ideas flew in the face of the dry fly thinking of the late nineteenth and early twentieth centuries and coupled with the fact that Skues was so remarkably successful with his 'new' methods, it was not surprising that considerable rancour broke out in the dry fly quarter. On occasion Skues was branded an infidel and many for and against fierce exchanges followed in the angling press.

Despite his detractors Skues managed consistent success with his new methods and as a skilled lawyer was well able to defend himself in the face of stiff opposition. In all truth his actual fishing tactics were not that dissimilar to working a dry fly as he would cast upstream with a short floating line and then carefully keep control of the nymph with raised rod tip until it reached his feet again whereupon another couple of steps upstream were taken and the fly cast out again. The nub of this casting method was not blind 'chuck it and chance it' wet fly rather it was to use an alternative method to dry fly angling when the dry was failing to tempt a visibly rising trout.

Typical nymph in the Skues mould

Basically Skues liked to be flexible in his fishing techniques using dry or wet fly when the case demanded. And it must be remembered that nymph fishing upstream was not necessarily the soft option as some of his detractors claimed, in fact it was and still is quite difficult to master especially in a fast current. However if he or she fishes eruditely, the upstream nymph fisher will often out-fish the upstream dry fly angler then and now.

Skues' ideas on fly tying also stand up to modern scrutiny. He noted the most effective hackle flies for river angling were the ones dressed with a 'kick' which pushed the head hackle slightly forward giving it a more life-like pulsing presentation in the water. This kick is essential for effective fishing upstream and stops the hackle flattening in the current. He may not have actually invented this technique of fly tying but he was one of the first to recognise its use on southern chalkstreams. In addition Skues took a principal lead in imitating aquatic trout food and concocted patterns to resemble freshwater shrimp, alder fly larvae and caddis pupa. Skues also propounded on the need for the fly to have 'a good entry' when fishing a fly in fast water. This meant a fly must swim in the water in a natural rather than awkwardly resisting way without 'carrying bubbles with it'. Skues thought an artificial should be dressed in such a way that it did not scare fish i.e. normally sparse and with a small head hackle which did not trap air. This appears in direct contradiction to the Irish Bumble theories later described by Kingsmill Moore (see Ireland) who rated the air and light carrying fibres of artificial flies as vitally important in their ability to attract trout. Skues also refused to concur with some of the convoluted dry fly dressing methods of the period. There is a lovely dig at the obsessions of exact imitation of insects so prevalent in the early twentieth century when he remarks in *The Way of a Trout with a Fly* that 'The imitation may be Impressionist, Cubist, Futurist, Pre Raphaelite or caricature. The commonest is caricature. It therefore catches most fish.' Great stuff...

The Netheravon School – Sawyer and Kite

The anglers of the interestingly named Netheravon School were followers of the principals of G M Skues however in many cases they actually honed and improved the great man's ideas on river nymph fishing. Between 1940 and 1960 Frank Sawyer, a water keeper based on the Netheravon stretch of the Avon in Hampshire, and his younger disciple Oliver Kite extended theories on angling with nymphs. Sawyer evolved and simplified Skues' theories of replica nymphs for different species of aquatic life and made more general nymph imitations which went on to be proved equally effective. His signature Sawyer's Pheasant Tail Nymph is known throughout the world today. Sawyer commented on this pattern that its success was due to the fact that 'it might well, in different sizes, be mistaken by fish for one of at least a dozen nymphs of various genus and species...' The Netheravon patterns were easy to make (few had wings or hackle) and easy to use giving a realistic presentation in the water when fished upstream.

Oliver Kite (1920-1968) followed closely in Sawyer's footsteps and between them they evolved a specific method of fishing their select nymph patterns. Instead of allowing the flies to drift down on a dead drift as Skues did these anglers developed what they called the 'induced take'. This technique involved a light twitch of the rod tip either up or to the side in order to impart a life-like swimming action to the underwater nymph. Kite argued this technique was necessary in order to let the fish see the nymph believing that trout feed on invertebrates according to how they move in the water rather than just because the artificial is tied in exactly the right colour and size. Kite wrote in his book *Nymph Fishing in Practice* that the angler should follow the dictum 'Aim to deceive your fish by offering it an imitation roughly resembling the natural nymph it is expecting to see at the level it would normally see it.' In addition he theorised that the nymph should be presented in such a way that 'it behaves as the fish is expecting it to behave'. Kite was equally adamant like Skues that an instant strike when a fish is felt or anticipated is in order to secure a catch, he said 'Know this; in dry fly fishing there are times when delay may be essential for effective striking, in nymph fishing you cannot afford the luxury of any delay'. To be able to strike effectively Kite advocated watching the nylon in order to see the little dip it takes when a trout moves away with the artificial nymph. This is great in meandering smooth streams but obviously much more difficult in fast broken water.

Thus both Kite and Sawyer switched angling thinking away from constructing the correct imitation and moved it toward the correct presentation. Not only that but they were quite free in their thinking as to where the correct presentation could be used. Instead of always casting to a visibly rising fish they found it completely acceptable to use the upstream induced take technique in likely looking trout holding areas. Sawyer pointed out in his book *Nymphs and the Trout* (1958) that these methods of nymphing were not indiscriminate flogging of the water, rather the upstream induced take technique could be used to search deeper trout lies. In pioneering these skills Sawyer and Kite opened up nymph fishing skills to a wider audience. Their development of quick sinking weighted nymph patterns was the precursor of the modern Czech Nymph and other deep fishing shrimp patterns. Sawyer's Killer Bug for example was probably the first in what has now become a long line of weighted nymph patterns.

Looking back to the 1960s might be considered a very recent past in English angling terms yet it is good to see that innovation in river fishing had not ceased. We owe Sawyer and Kite a debt of gratitude for bringing versatility into English river fishing which had up until then been stuck in a totally dry or totally wet fly approach.

River Sea Trout Fishing and the Falkus Influence

English sea trout river angling saw rather scant coverage during the nineteenth and early twentieth centuries. As in Scotland, the English preferred to catch salmon rather than trout in their rivers. In 1899 Lord Grey remarked that 'sea trout in a large salmon river are not of much more account than grouse in a deer forest and are even looked upon as a nuisance when they are running and take a salmon fly freely.' However he does acknowledge that first rate sport could be had on light tackle for fresh sea trout during a spate in July and August especially when the river was high and just beginning to fall. Equally he seemed to enjoy the test of finding trout in challenging conditions though interestingly he did the majority of it in Scotland rather than England.

Prior to the 1960s English writers like Dawson, Bluett and Grey made the main literary contributions on their nation's basic techniques for sea trout. They recorded using either trout flies or larger skinny salmon flies especially at night and on a sunk line but in all truth not many real distinctions were drawn between river sea trout fishing and salmon angling. It was not until 1962 that the prerequisite skills for sea trout were fully recognised in England as a separate art. It was in this year distinguished fisherman and naturalist Hugh Falkus published *Sea Trout Fishing* (followed on by a much enlarged second edition in 1975) and his writings were to take the English sea trout world by storm. Falkus must be credited with putting forward groundbreaking ideas which influenced and altered the course of migratory trout fishing not only in England but across the whole of the UK. His practical yet innovative approach to sea trout angling did much to further techniques in the hunting of migratory trout. He was an angler never afraid to nail his colours to the mast and his literary efforts went a long way in reversing some ill thought theories on sea trout feeding behaviour particularly when the fish are in the river environment as opposed to being at sea.

It should also be remembered that it was largely Falkus who swept away some earlier presumptions on how to catch migratory trout particularly the idea put forward by other English anglers of his era that these fish would only take particular artificial flies which imitated a natural hatch going on in the river. A pedantic matching of the hatch to catch migratory trout Falkus stated was 'nonsense and anyone believing it need not feel surprised when catches are light'. Instead he suggested that the sea trout took an angler's fly or lure largely like a mountaineer climbs the hill simply 'because it is there'. Falkus suggested the angler should adopt a practical approach to fly construction making flies which elicit a curious or aggressive response from the fish as well as a feeding one. In this he rather followed earlier Scottish loch sea trout ploys which involved using big attractor patterns. However his revised novel versions of sea trout flies particularly 'Surface Lures', 'Medicines' and 'Secret Weapons' went further than the old traditional sea trout patterns developed on Scottish lochs. These are further discussed in the Welsh angling section for the anglers of that country have embraced Falkus' concepts with particular gusto and as a consequence they will be dealt with there.

It has been said that Falkus was at times an outspoken and controversial character who did not suffer fools gladly. If this is so he merely followed in many other English angling greats' footsteps – the Halford and Skues camps were not short of the odd sharp word or two either. Falkus can easily be forgiven for any curmudgeoness as few modern writers come close to his lucid recording of sea trout tactics and techniques. The skills first developed by Falkus at his beloved Cragg Cottage on the border Esk in Cumbria are now in universal use across the UK and further afield and in sea trout angling terms we have much to thank him for.

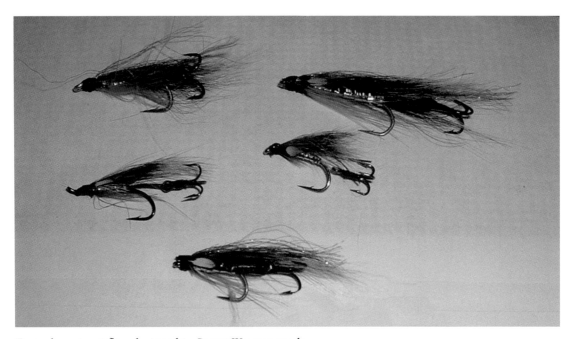

Typical sea trout flies designed in Secret Weapon mode

Modern English River Fishing

In some ways English river fishing appears to have come a long way from the days of wet fly and fishing 'at the top'. Yet for all the modernisations of tackle, the current techniques remain comparable to the old. Today we still have wet fly designs which are remarkably similar to the first ever constructed. We still have English anglers keenly using soft hackle wet flies and fishing up and across in the northern counties and there are still dry fly purists lurking on the southern chalkstreams. Exponents of Skues' upstream nymph are common and the weighted nymphs or bugs first pioneered by Sawyer and Kite are consistently popular. Those who fish for river sea trout will still readily use a Falkus recommendation before any other more modern creation.

Regarding dry fly angling, yes we have absorbed some excellent techniques from Europe and America especially involving fly construction, for example dry flies like Adams and Wulff now adorn many an English fly box. And while fly lines and rods are far more sophisticated, the essence of all types of river angling remains good presentation, Walton knew this in the 1600s and the same tactics hold true many centuries later. Whether you concoct a wonderful exact replica of a Halford or Skues pattern or go for a minimalist wisp of feather to catch trout, you need to present the fly to the fish in a way which does not scare them. In some ways it is extraordinary that the concentrated careful stalking of river trout while exploring likely looking trout holding areas is still the principal skill we all have to master just as it was aeons ago for the grand masters. Threading a delicate line through the undergrowth with the aim of putting a fly near a waiting trout in a natural but controlled way without terrifying him, is still the first prerequisite in successful river fishing.

What has changed perhaps is the colossal degree of dogma associated with English river fly fishing. No longer are there quite so many camps and cliques complete with arched eyebrows and tut tuts when an angler switches say from dry fly to nymph. Instead we have generally adopted a more flexible approach and this is a very welcome advance. However do remember that this liberalisation has not extended to all rivers for even in the twenty-first century certain rivers in southern England only allow upstream dry fly or a combination of upstream nymph and dry fly fishing. Part of this might be due to the small size of some of the chalkstream beats which mean you walk down to the end of it and fish back upstream to your car and the whole exercise may take only half a morning or an evening. Fishing restrictions may also be due to fishing pressure. This means you are fishing over trout which have seen many other anglers' flies and lines and it can be said that upstream casting at least keeps you the predator, out of sight and makes for less wary trout.

I like to compare English river fishing with a hearty oak tree. The roots are deep and stretch way back to Walton and Cotton and before, the branches have spread out to encompass the likes of Skues and Halford and Sawyer, the leaves have been nourished by modern influences from both home and abroad, yet the core trunk remains solid, trim and true – nice thought anyway.

| *Stillwater fishing has become increasingly popular since the early 1900s*

Chapter 9

ENGLISH LAKE FISHING

Early Days on the Lakes

In much the same way that Scotland's loch fishing failed to attract much specific literary attention in the 1800s, lake and reservoir fishing in England have similarly few early bookish masterpieces to their credit. Oblique references to lake fishing were made during the nineteenth century; some raved about the scenery in the Lake District more than they did the practical capture of trout while others discussed the merits of rearing trout in small ponds, however the practicalities of lake angling skills were not much recorded. Unlike English river fishing which had by that time amassed libraries of tomes on the subject, there was little writing of substance on the necessary techniques for English stillwater angling until the turn of the twentieth century. Prior to that if the techniques for lake angling were mentioned at all they were added as an aside rather than having a whole book devoted to them.

However what information we can glean from those early writings makes interesting reading. For a start there are definite similarities between Scottish and English thoughts on the fishing skills which might be required for lakes. In Scotland angling doyen W C Stewart around 1850 had already branded loch fishing as tiresomely monotonous, effectively making many Scottish anglers believe for far too long that loch angling offered poor sport. In England fellow anglers appeared almost as quick to put forward similar prejudices. A lot of this discrimination seems to stem from the larger heavier dressed types of flies used for loch/lake fishing. The Marquess of Granby writing in 1897 was dismissive on lake angling stating pointedly 'I can only deal generally with this branch of trout fishing for it is not as if it were pursued with artificial flies tied after the likeness of natural insects, in which case much more might be said on the subject'. It would appear that in those early days English fishermen were quick to elevate river fishing to a separate pure art form and quite undeservedly push stillwater lake angling into the lesser realms of technical skill.

Thankfully this blinkered attitude was forced to change when in the early 1900s two crucial events happened in the trout fishing world. First the cumulative effect of industrial pollution on many of England's trout streams meant that sustained environmental damage had indiscriminately rendered much of both the working man and gentleman's river trout fishing almost to nothing. Hence there were lots of keen trout anglers with nowhere to fish. The second important event was the construction of many large reservoirs starting in the late 1800s and early 1900s, with many originally smaller lakes being dammed and considerably enlarged to form water containment areas. Reservoirs ranging from a small acreage to vast sheets of water remain dotted across England with the continued purpose of supplying water to large centres of conurbation like Manchester, Bristol, Birmingham, Sheffield. Thus much of English lake angling fell under the control of the local water authorities (usually termed in the early days the 'Corporation', and reservoirs like Rutland, Grantham, Ravensthorpe and Blagdon were opened up to the public for the purposes of general recreation and in particular, fishing. The water authorities became responsible for the general management of the reservoir and looked after the hire of boats, stocked the waters and provided bailiff services. In return the fishers using the reservoirs would pay appropriate permit fees as either local or visiting anglers. In addition national rod licence fees, which go toward the national upkeep of watercourses, could (and still can) be paid at the water itself which greatly assisted fee collection, see the Appendix. A number of the larger 'new' lakes had their own hatcheries built adjacent to them and this allowed stock to be reared locally. Where there was thought to be a diminishing wild trout population, new fish usually in the form of the quicker grown rainbow, could then be introduced for the benefit of the paying customers i.e. the anglers.

The opening up of many new waters from the early 1900s was a tremendous boost for anglers displaced from their polluted streams and when the big reservoirs took off fishing on them was welcomed like manna from heaven. The story does not end there however as in the latter half of the twentieth century enterprising landowners, realising that reservoir angling was becoming so popular, set about developing any possible containment of water they had on their grounds often leasing it out to potentially interested parties to manage and promote. Thus many more small stillwaters were created not as water supplies but essentially as sport fisheries. Anything from small ponds to disused quarries and gravel pits were up for renovation. Streams were diverted, areas flooded and green banked and fish species introduced with the sole purpose of what has now become known as 'put and take' angling. Often casting platforms are built out into the water to allow anglers to gain distance without entangling their fly lines in surrounding bushes or trees. Car parks, club houses and toilets were built in situ, creating comfort angling at its best. These small fisheries have thrived and given careful management can produce a reasonable income for those involved.

First Lake Flies

The earliest patterns used in earnest on English lakes appear to be derived from winged wet flies first constructed for flowing rather than still water. Patterns like the February Red or the Alder Fly, can be traced back to Cotton's time if not a good deal earlier and it can be assumed that these lake flies together with many like them were simply transferred from trout river fishing to the lakes. Earl Hodgson's book *Trout Fishing* (1904) has colour plate illustrations of established lake patterns from the preceding century and virtually all of these bar the Black Palmer or Red Palmer are winged wet flies. It is interesting that Hodgson gives reasonable support to lake fishing flies and skills for at that time he appears to be in the English minority. By the late 1800s with the dry fly revolution in full swing, many English society anglers began to scoff at the generations of 'old faithful' wet flies derisively labelling them unfashionable 'fancy flies' or 'general attractor' patterns not made as something to delicately match an exact hatch.

This swing in the social trends attached to English trout fishing and fly tying in particular is further vividly illustrated by comparing the writings of Francis with those of the Marquess of Granby. In his 1867 book *Book on Angling* respected angler Francis wrote of (unfortunately nameless) lake flies with teal wings and gold or silver ribbed bodies which he described as very effective on stillwaters. Thrty years later the Marquess of Granby also describes them as 'efficacious' but at the same time qualifies his opinion by further describing these lake flies as 'utterly unlike living ones'. The latter's words appear to echo several other English (and Scottish) anglers' opinions on the status of lake/loch flies by the late 1800s. The old lake wet fly patterns established in the early 1800s were larger, bushier and more colourful than the flies used for river fishing. Quite simply they just did not fit in with 'nouveau' fly tying theories of Halford et al which centred on small, sparse and delicate dry flies made with the right colour and shape to exactly imitate a currently hatching insect.

In the past lake flies were often dismissed as too fancy to match the hatch

In addition lake flies were in some cases thought to be imitating young fish like minnows, something which was at the very least tantamount to heresy in the blossoming 'purist' camp. A good example of this small fish imitation is the Alexandra fly which was first introduced into English fishing around 1860. Unlike other more vague histories of stillwater patterns this fly has a definite pedigree. First tied as 'The Lady of the Lake' it was renamed in honour of Princess Alexandra who may or may not have caught lake trout with it. The secret of its success is its silvery body, peacock herl, greenish wing and long red tail, and if that didn't imitate a small fleeing fish what did! The Butcher is a fly of similar design made with equal intention of imitating small aquatic prey intent on escaping capture by a large trout however this fly may have been made first for use on a river before ending up on the lake.

Fortunately, despite the pedantic views of nineteenth century society on lake flies, stillwater fishing survived and when the big reservoirs got off the ground in the early twentieth century many anglers were perfectly happy to up sticks with their existing river patterns like the Greenwell's Glory, Grouse and Claret or the March Brown and fish with them on the lakes. It's interesting that there must have been some exchange of stillwater tactics across the border for a goodly number of Scottish patterns turned up in English fly boxes and vice versa. The Butcher fly is thought to originate from Tunbridge Wells yet it is one of the most successful Scottish loch flies ever devised, similarly the Invicta first made by Ogden of Cheltenham is a supremely successful Scottish loch fly. The Greenwell's was made for a Scots river, the Tweed, yet it was in common use all over England by the late 1800s. The Black Palmer used for centuries on Scottish lochs might be derived from a seventeenth century Cotton pattern and so the list goes on.

Modern Lake Patterns

Unlike in Scotland where traditional loch flies and variants thereof are still in reasonably widespread use, English lake flies have seen a huge transformation in their design. The old traditional patterns do remain in modern fly fishing practice but both the flies and the anglers who use them now form the minority rather than the majority of the English stillwater angling population. From the 1960s onward a surge in the popularity of reservoir fishing either as a competitive sport or as a leisure pastime has meant a wide range of new patterns have been introduced to the fly box. These modern lake flies are principally made for the purpose of catching stillwater rainbow trout rather than browns and over the past fifty years or so there has been a huge growth in their number. The first nouveau lake flies fell into the categories of long shank hook lures of different hue like the Jersey Herd, Ace of Spades, the Appetiser and the Whisky Fly. These may well have been copied from American patterns as the anglers of the USA had been making flies dressed as lures since the early 1900s. These were followed by weighted quick sinking flies like Lead-heads, Beasties and Dog Nobblers and following on from

A modern mix

them came a range of bouyant lures like Booby Nymphs. If certain traditional patterns made the old trout fishing doyens squirm, this colourful nouveau selection would send them into an apoplectic spin in their graves.

Progress in stillwater flies does not stop at the lure design however as modern English reservoir anglers now also use a broad selection of slightly more subtle nymph patterns in order to catch rainbows and to a lesser extent brown trout. With roots in ancient sparse river patterns these 'new' nymphs made an easy transition to lake work (see Developing Lake Tactics). These lake nymphs are designed to fish at various depths and the use of different modern materials in fly construction has helped achieve this goal. Some are made for use in the surface film, principally midge imitations with names like Buzzers, Suspenders, Footballers, Corixas, Pheasant Tails and so on. Mayfly, Stonefly, Shrimp and Damsel fly nymphs are all being represented and are fished more or less as the natural insect. In addition weighted nymphs are now used to great effect on stillwaters with nymphs like the Gold Ribbed Hare's Ear or the Sedge Pupa reinvented with a little weighted bead at their head to help fast sinking. These flies can be said to represent a turn back to more imitative forms of fishing rather than basic lure stripping.

Developing Lake Tactics

It is somewhat ironic that those early angling writers who were so dismissive of what they saw as highly unfashionable lake flies circa the 1890s actually offer some reasonably practical advice as to how to fish them. Just as W C Stewart offered fine advice for loch fishing, Granby puts forward sensible tactics for the lakes suggesting trying every likely part of the lake whether trout are rising or not and that the best places to fish are the margins where they 'abut on the deep water and round rushes or weed beds'. Granby also says that fishing will be productive in the region of 'Whatever causes a break in the surface of the lake...whether it be a point of a rock, fallen branch or anything else which causes a swirl in the water...collecting together food of some description thereby attracting the trout to its vicinity'. In addition he describes changing (wet) fly sizes according to the degree of ruffle on the water surface and that the flies should be worked in the water in opposite fashion to letting the fly float quietly on a river. All of this advice was basically sound and can be safely followed today in traditional fishing.

Early styles of English reservoir/lake fly fishing appear very similar in execution to Scottish loch style angling. According to Ernest Phillips in his book *Trout in Lakes and Reservoirs* (1914) the established skills at that time (but obviously brought forward from previous years) centred on using teams of the aforementioned traditional patterns. Phillips favoured flies like the Wickham's, Hare's Ear, March Brown, Silver Sedge, Zulu or the Greenwell's Glory. These were fished in teams with patterns rotated according to the season, for example the Zulu might be fished on the top dropper mid season but on the point at the end of the angling year. He makes some interesting distinctions as to how many flies were used in reservoir angling stating that 'In Scotland the custom is to use four at once, on the English Lake District the number is three and on some (southern England) reservoirs where the habit of using very large flies has grown, two (flies) are sufficient'. Phillips indicates the tactics of fishing flies were broadly similar 'loch style' on a short floating line with the medium paced retrieve and a dibble of the top dropper before lift off were then in common use on most if not all of the main English reservoirs like Chew, Blagdon and Ravensthorpe. Rods were at that time cane or greenheart and had to be according to Phillips 'with sufficient bone in them to cast well out in the teeth of a gale'. He normally used a rod around 10 to 11 feet in length and this would appear standard equipment in the early part of the twentieth century. Although Phillips describes boat fishing he implies that bank fishing was also common and that these tactics were applicable to either situation.

Thus the old skills of a slightly anglicised 'loch style' remained in common practice for the first half of the twentieth century until the rainbow revolution on the English reservoirs took off from the early 1960s and never looked back.

Importance of Competition Fishing on English Reservoirs

Just as we have seen a definite revolution in English fly design with the pre 1960s traditional flies bearing little or no relation to those that followed on, so too can we see new different skills growing up alongside and sometimes overtaking the old. This evolution in reservoir tactics is almost certainly due to the popularity of competition fishing. This began in the 1930s but only really took off post 1970s reaching amazing heights of popularity during the 1980s when Benson and Hedges sponsored various club competitions. The quarry for these events was nearly always the rainbow trout rather than the brown and competitive anglers had (and still have) to try and catch trout no matter what the prevailing conditions were doing. This led to a wide range of ploys being used and in some cases, there was a move away from the old simplicity of traditional 'top of the water' floating line skills. From the 1970s onward technology had to race forward to keep up with English competition fishers' demands. A much wider variety of lines like heavy quick sinking Hi Ds, sink/ghost tips, shooting heads, intermediates came into production and these developments in theory meant the angler could fish at most depths and at much greater distances from the shore if required. In addition a much more diverse range of fly tying materials, anything from epoxy resin to ethafoam and from glitter dust to flashabou complete with stick on eyes can be employed, meant that many new flies meant to catch rainbow trout have come on the market.

At the same time better carbon fibre technology meant rods were being made which could cope with the new weighty fly lines. This was probably just as well as more power and strength was desperately needed to launch some of the more heavyweight ones! Casting skills too were adapted and techniques like the double haul which gave extra distance to the normal overhead cast became increasingly popular with the bank angler. The competition scene flourished from one end of England to the other. Just as Scotland had its 'Loch Leven influence' the same can be said for those big English reservoirs like Blagdon, Chew, Rutland or Grantham where fishers pushed both equipment and techniques into new territories in order to win competitions. Fishing against the clock purely with the purpose of bettering fellow anglers' bags may not be everyone's idea of sporting fishing, yet it is doubtful if so much could have been achieved in reservoir angling if those events ranging from local club to international competitions had not been so popular.

Lure Fishing

Although the Americans appear to have been doing it since the early 1900s using streamer and bucktail patterns, lure fishing in England only got serious from around 1950 onward. One prominent stillwater angler of that period, Tom Ivens, produced a fly called the 'Jersey Herd' and this was perhaps the forerunner of the many lure designs which have followed. Apart from the fact that lure fishing is almost always done for rainbow trout rather than browns, two aspects set angling with lures apart from traditional loch style methods. The first is the method of fishing which involves using a sinking rather than floating line and retrieving it with short and long dashing pulls on the line to make the fly (often used singly rather than in

Blagdon Lake prime competition territory

a team) simulate a darting fish. This method, often known as stripping, tweaks the fly along quickly beneath the surface and differs from the rhythmic top of the water medium paced retrieve often associated with loch style. An adaptation of this is the strip and hang method usually employed while boat fishing. It involves casting the line out and letting the flies sink down while taking up the slack as the boat drifts down in the wind. Once the flies are down as far as you think appropriate you start the retrieve in long draws followed by a fast retrieve while lifting the rod arm high until the top dropper appears and then drop the rod tip down once more before lifting off to cast again. The idea behind this is to make the flies dip up and down as a small fish might do and it can be very effective in the early season when trout are feeding sporadically and at different depths.

The second aspect is the common use in lure fishing of a heavier long shank fly which solely imitates a small fleeing fish fry, some of the old traditional patterns like the Butcher or the Alexandra already imitated tiny fish but these were used as part of a team of flies. The tying of larger heavier flies (anything from size 4 up to size 10) on long shank hooks with modern materials like chenille or marabou was a deliberate departure from the old brown trout patterns and a definite attempt to tempt only the stocked rainbows of the big reservoirs. Lures like the Dog Nobbler, White Marabou or the Floating Fry teamed with fast sinking lines like the Hi Speed Hi D meant that a whole new range of depths could be covered by the angler. The basic method of stripping these lures back sometimes with a side to side motion to imitate fish in panic might be looked upon as rather like spinning a lure or a plug. In this way the 'roly poly' came into use. This involved placing the rod under the arm and rotating the

105

line back hand over fist to generate immense speed with the lure racing back through the water towards the angler in a straight line. This method appears to be derived partly from the old Scottish gillies' trick of paying out the fly line a good way behind the boat and then rowing upwind so that the fly travels unnaturally fast through the water some distance off. It also bears similarity to 'trolling under power' which is illegal on many English waters as the fly ends up moving at such a pace it might be being used under engine power! Roly poly has little or no skill in it and at some waters it has been outlawed.

In addition to changing the method of retrieving, the employment of large bouyant lures akin to the original American-made Muddler Minnow tweaked along on an intermediate or slow sinking line instead of a traditional floater, seems at times to be a successful method. On occasion rainbow trout will chase after the bobbing fly like fish possessed. A favourite 'fly' used in this odd combination is the Booby which first appeared on the rainbow reservoir scene around the 1980s. As the name suggests this is an adaptive method of fly tying which adds two balls of foam trapped in stocking mesh to either side of the fly head. Virtually any large nymph or lure pattern can be adapted in this way. Whether this is fly fishing as we know it I leave you to judge but there are occasions when trout are in aggressive mood that bouyant lures works well.

A slightly more subtle form of lure fishing involves the adaptation of traditional patterns like say an Invicta with pearly, sparkly or flashy materials. These additions are normally in the form of a flashy rib, head or tail and are aimed at bringing extra brightness to an otherwise fairly drab coloured fly. This fly tying tactic has produced legions of variants (sometimes collectively known as Flashers) from about the early 1980s onward and still does today. In some cases a little more sparkle can indeed attract trout particularly rainbows, yet in others they seem to fail miserably. I can only hazard a guess as to why this is in that over dressing flies originally tied to represent a particular shape of insect or fish may take away the shape and the natural movement of a prey the trout recognise and replace it with a hugely overdressed, unnatural looking lump. In other words a subtle twinkly add-on is fine however a great bunch of fluorescent light gathering silver and gold may be over kill and scare fish far more than attract them.

All types of lure fishing have enjoyed considerable popularity from the 1960s onwards and remain highly prevalent in English reservoir fishing today especially late in the season when small perch or roach fry are profuse and rainbow trout gorge themselves silly on them.

Nymph and Buzzer Fishing on Lakes

The first types of nymphs used on lakes were almost certainly those brought over from river angling. Pheasant Tails, Hare's Ears, Olive Nymphs as well as those lightly hackled flies like the Partridge and Orange or Snipe and Purple made an easy transition to stillwaters and these traditional patterns are still very popular in lake fishing in the twenty-first century. However in addition to the original flies, slightly different designs of nymph came into being from the late 60s onwards. Lake anglers started paying much more attention to the trout's preoccupation with midge feeding. Patterns were devised to imitate the different stages starting with larvae (also known as bloodworm) then to pupae and on through emerging pupae which are stuck sub surface, right to devising a pattern for the surface emerged midge. Winged adult midges which have taken flight (also known as Duckfly in Ireland and sometimes as 'Blae and Blacks' in Scotland) could be imitated by nouveau tyings like those constructed with Cul de Canard or by using traditional patterns like the Snipe and Purple or the Black Pennell. Each stage had a slightly different type of imitation made for it and these nymphs have also become collectively known as Buzzers. Thus there are flies with names like Emerger Buzzers or Suspender Buzzers and these new patterns have to some extent overtaken the older designs.

It is interesting that anglers on one of the first major English reservoirs to be opened up for public fishing, Blagdon near Bristol in Somerset, also had a hand in developing some of the first midge imitations. The Blagdon Buzzer devised by Dr H A Bell was a fly made to represent a midge pupa and it is likely that this pattern was one of the first stillwater flies to be used specifically for midge imitation (see also the section on Blagdon Lake). Though the importance of midge had also been recognised in Scotland on similarly rich waters like Loch Leven, Malloch circa 1909 made several references to trout gorging themselves with bloodworm in Leven, it appears it was the English who first decided upon constructing various more exact patterns rather than opting for general purpose traditional flies.

Bearing in mind nymph and buzzer fishing on stillwaters only really became popular in the latter half of the twentieth century, methods of working nymphs have changed little and follow broadly similar tactics. All are fished at a much slower pace than the rhythmical cast and retrieve of loch style and in some cases the flies do little except hang in a pre-selected layer of water. When fishing midge larvae, which are tied so sparse they are often little more than a twist of varnished floss and a tiny tuft of herl at the head, you want to have them working near the lake bottom on an intermediate or full sinking line depending on water depth. The idea is to use a team of midge larvae imitations (normally two or three flies) on a long leader sometimes up to 20ft or so, cast out and let the line sink down before twitching the flies back in a slow jerky motion to imitate a small squirming bloodworm. In very deep water a heavier weighted nymph can be employed on the point to draw the nymphs down. Occasionally in shallower margins a weighted top dropper is used on a long leader with a midge larvae pattern set on the point. In this case the heavier fly sinks first and draws both

CDC Buzzers

the flies down slowly with it. Both these tactics make the bloodworm imitations appear to be swimming jerkily about at the correct depth and hopefully a big trout will intercept them.

Midge larvae fishing differs slightly from angling with midge pupae imitations as the natural insect drifts rather lifelessly in the lake often in large numbers but at changing but specific depth. This has led to anglers using 'counting down' tactics in the hope of hitting the right depth where the fish are feeding on the pupae. Fishers use a fast sink line with a strong leader and count down how many seconds it takes to hit the bottom and then try fishing at different lesser time intervals hopefully to come up with gold at the correct depth. If that sounds too complicated, a long leader up to 18ft or so can be used and a team of midge pupae imitations fished very slowly with a figure of eight retrieve. The important point to remember here is that you are fishing a dead drift. Rather than imparting life to the fly as is done in traditional loch style you want it to look as if it's hanging still or drifting down 'on the drop' through imaginary layers of water. Speaking from experience, English reservoir specialists do this second nature, but seasoned 'loch stylers' find it difficult not to automatically move the flies. One Midlands reservoir angler Arthur Cove became a legendary expert at this type of dead drift fishing inching back flies with a figure of eight retrieve and is said to be able to spot a take by watching the entry point of the leader in the water. If he saw the leader go down he struck immediately and secured hundreds if not thousands of trout by this method. He devised the Cove Nymph for this type of painstaking work, a fly very similar to Skues' Pheasant Tail Nymph.

Continuing on the midge theme, for it plays a huge part in lake and reservoir fishing, sub surface and surface emergers like the Black Emerger Buzzer, the Shipman's Buzzer or the Bucknall Footballer are also worked slowly with the idea of imitating buzzers on or just about to emerge from the water's surface film. Teams of two or three of these types of flies are used sometimes with a top dropper dry fly attached as a sight indicator so that when it moves it means a trout is mouthing the buzzer beneath the surface. If the occasion merits it, a weighted nymph can be placed on the point almost as an 'anchor' while the other nymphs lie at different depths below the surface. This method is sometimes known as the 'sacrificial nymph' meaning that the trout are not expected to take the deepest point fly rather they are likely to intercept the mid or top dropper at the depth they are feeding.

It is a bit like splitting hairs to say whether the trout takes the slightly different type of emerger patterns because they are atop the water surface, stuck in surface film struggling to free themselves from the midge shuck or still slowly travelling upward. Personally there are times when I don't think such minute detail is absolutely necessary, rather I feel it's often the angler's method of presentation which wins the day. Slow almost imperceptible movement of the flies just to stay in touch is the key to success with any type of imitative nymph fishing and give them their due, English reservoir specialists seem particularly good at it!

Dry Fly on the Lakes

There is a defined split in the use of dry fly on English lakes. Before the rainbow revolution and the leaps and bounds made by competitive fishing, early dry fly fishing on stillwaters was confined to large bushy general imitations. Trouble is these were not called dry flies despite the fact their heavier bushy dressings would have undoubtedly made them very bouyant. Large Red or Black Palmers, Mayflies and similar were frequently employed yet unlike R C Bridgett in Scotland circa 1920 who made frequent reference to using dry fly angling in many different situations on stillwater, English lake angler Ernest Phillips circa 1914 only makes reference to using a single dry fly in a flat calm. This tactic he thought was rather a risky business as he felt the lone floating fly might put off more fish than it would actually take – a strange assumption.

Users of dry fly on lakes were in the minority throughout the first half of the twentieth century, even in the 1970s famous anglers like Tom Ivens, a reservoir specialist, dismissed stillwater dry fly and plumped instead for all forms of wets. It seemed to take an interminably long time but finally in the 1990s John Gale was to write that on reservoirs like Grantham, top competition anglers were using the dry fly as a regular weapon. Creative fly tying brought us many new or revised dry fly patterns notably Sedges, Daddies and Hoppers. Of the former there are now legions of patterns ranging from the G&H Sedge to the Silver Sedge with literally hundreds of variants in between. The Great Red Sedge tied by Dave Collyer is a particularly effective one and a reservoir standard. It looks very fish attractive and relatively realistic when placed beside newer reservoir dry flies like Sedgehogs, CDC Bubble Sedges and Flexi Floss Daddies. Wonderful names but basically little more than variants on a dry fly theme.

Versions of The Daddy (also known as Crane Fly) have also been around since the 1960s, eminent anglers Geoffrey Bucknall and Richard Walker both made fine dry imitations, but today we have a greatly expanded range incorporating super bouyant materials like deer hair or Cul de Canard. Hoppers (smaller more straggly different coloured versions of daddy long

The modern lake fisher's fly box contains a healthy mix of dries, nymphs and wets

legs) were a later invention created by anglers from the Bristol reservoirs of Blagdon and Chew. These patterns greased up and fished dry in teams of three on floating lines proved outstandingly successful and the use of Hoppers quickly surpassed the older more precisely tied Daddies. These more modern general imitative flies were produced in a wide range of colours with red, brown, amber, fiery brown, claret and black all being employed. Fished on long leaders and floating lines they were a truly innovative pattern and now few reservoir anglers are without a few in their fly box.

Today English lake anglers have incorporated many different dry flies both from America and Europe and the old prejudices of not using dry fly on reservoirs are largely forgotten.

Drifts in the Boat

Unlike in Ireland and Scotland, dapping on English lakes never seems to have gained any favour and it is a rare occurrence to see it being used. The first methods boat anglers appeared to use were primarily related to the time honoured Scottish loch style method of fishing for brown trout by drifting a boat down wind with the boat set parallel and the anglers with their backs to the wind. The earliest mention of English boat angling I can find relates to a strange 'over the stern' method of drifting a boat and is mentioned in Granby's *Trout* in 1897. Here it is recommended that the boatman takes the boat upwind then stops and lets it drift back stern first with the angler standing or sitting in the stern and casting from there. The boatman has to keep a strong arm on the oars to stop the boat drifting too fast and allow the angler time to cover as much water as possible. Apart from anything else, this seems to be a rather dangerous method of boat fishing and not surprisingly it is rarely used today.

When rainbow reservoir fishing came to the fore anglers devised other methods of working flies from a boat. Thus we now also have fishing at anchor, back drifting and Northampton style being employed to catch trout just as much as the old traditional loch style drift. Fishing at anchor (an illegal method in Scotland) is highly common on many English reservoirs and the main aim is to anchor up so that both anglers get a chance to fish with the wind behind over a likely looking spot such as the mouth of a small bay or over a shallow shelf near the margins. By dropping an anchor the boat maintains its position even in a strong wind and allows anglers to explore all fishy possibilities. Nymph and buzzer fishing is particularly effective at anchor as the flies can be fished virtually static and allowed to waft gently just like the natural insect would do in any underwater current but lure fishers also use the anchor to allow them to strip lures back over likely lies in the hope of getting a smash take.

Back drifting is a strange, slightly dubious method of paying out line behind the drifting boat and into the wind rather than the traditional front of the boat style of fishing. There is not much casting involved and this method bears more than a bit of a resemblance to trolling. The angler uses the power of the wind to move his flies in the water as the boats drifts down. This method is of benefit to disabled anglers who are unable to cast. 'Northampton style' boat angling (also known as fishing on the rudder) is also a controversial method of fishing and it has been banned on certain waters in England. The boat is taken upwind and then turned to drift down again bow first. This method is actually the reverse of the early drift style mentioned by Granby, in the 1800s the stern went first now it's the bow! The anglers sit facing into the wind and each casts across the wind from either side of the boat. The wind pushes the boat along and the anglers' lines swing slowly round in an arc of sorts sometimes known as side swiping. A strong lure rod with 9 – 11 fast sink line is often used with this method together with a selection of lures. As Northampton style, like back drifting, also rather imitates trolling it is not much seen in Scotland and Ireland.

Stillwater fishing on the Isle of Man

Small Stillwater Fishing

There are so many small stocked stillwaters scattered across England which are fished primarily from the bank it is worth pointing out the most productive tactics. This type of fishing is sometimes described as stew pond angling because in most cases all the trout present will be introduced rather than native fish. Today across the UK we see numerous small fisheries stocked with browns, rainbows as well as amongst other more exotic imports like brook trout, blue trout, Apache trout and so on. Unfortunately it is often said that on fisheries which are intensively stocked to the point of bursting at the seams, all that the angler requires in the skills department is an ability to appear on the bank and chuck a fly on to the water. Hatchery-bred trout fed on nothing but pellets will race to take hold of your hook and hey presto, mission accomplished! I cannot say I endorse these high density stocking policies. By exclusively promoting 'easy' trout fishing, the fishery managers responsible are actually encouraging their angling clientele to develop great and ultimately unrealistic expectations of the size and number of trout they think they can catch in any given fishing situation. For obvious reasons 'stew pond' fishermen are less able to build up skills which are translatable to the capture of a wild indigenous fish. Effectively they miss out on some great challenges of trout fishing and may really struggle when visiting wild waters of any sort, flowing or still. Basically stew pond fishing is all right if that is as high as you set your goals, personally I like and need much more of a contest.

That said, if you choose your small stillwater carefully with a little prior research particularly on stocking densities you can still have a wonderfully enjoyable and testing day in pleasant country surroundings and there can be little wrong with that. Many of these little lakes are spring fed and as a consequence the water can be gin clear. This means a careful approach coupled with delicate casting, quiet stalking of trout while keeping a low profile are definite requirements for this type of angling. Fly lines are either floating, intermediate or slow sink and flies range from small dries through lures to nymphs and wets. Because of the small size of the water trout are likely to cruise around following set paths and the observant angler can usually suss this out quite quickly. Polaroids aid fish spotting considerably and tactics often come down to trying to intercept a moving fish or casting to a definite rise. Though it might not be quite as demanding as big lake angling there is a certain appeal to this type of commercial fishing in miniature.

Modern Lake Angling

From sketchy early beginnings where it often played second fiddle to river angling, English lake fishing has come a very long way. Today we see a huge variety of lake crafts and customs and these changes can largely be put down to the popularity of rainbow trout angling which has to a great extent overtaken brown trout traditions. Lake fishing skills now encompass anything from the vaguely traditional to the ultra modern. In particular anglers making use of so many diverse new fly tying materials means that lake flies have taken on many more new guises from lure to nymph and from old traditional to a vast assortment of modern buzzers. To fish these the angler is now equipped with an equally wide range of lines and rods. The larger lakes and reservoirs are dominated (though not exclusively) by boat angling aficionados while small stocked stillwaters will see legions of bank fishers especially at weekends.

If any comparison can be made of English stillwater angling say with neighbouring Scotland or Ireland it must be noted that there is a much more commercial flavour to fishing English stillwaters. Any cursory glance at a map of the British Isles shows that Scotland and Ireland lead the way on natural lochs/loughs with thousands upon thousands dotted across their combined landscapes. This means fishing is generally more easily obtained there, uncrowded and freely available to visitors. In contrast England and Wales have far fewer large water bodies yet have a much larger population of anglers sometimes having to compete to find space to fish. To meet fishers' demands, stillwaters have therefore had to become tightly run enterprises. It must also be said that English lake angling in general has benefited from the rod licence system which does not exist in Scotland. Anglers paying for these licences make the authorities accountable for managing their lakes (and rivers) in return for the permit fee. There is no such accountability for the management of Scotland's watercourses and this makes sustainable management of fish populations that much more difficult there.

Basically with English stillwater angling it might cost you a bit more but you will have more facilities on hand, a management system in place and in most cases you get what you pay for, a point worth remembering when tackling this country's stillwaters.

Chapter 10

Cornerstones of English Trout Fishing

With a history stretching back to the days of the *Treatise* in the1400s it is a well nigh impossible task to pick but a few examples of waters which can be described as essential cornerstones in English angling. We have seen so much come of English fishing in general with huge advances in both river and lake techniques being made over several centuries. The introduction of dry fly, upstream wets, chalkstream tactics, soft hackle flies and the applied use of nymphs on rivers would never have come about had not we had such determined pioneers of English angling and in this we owe them a huge debt. Similarly in stillwater fishing we have seen a transformation of tactics brought about largely from the influence of competitive twentieth century rainbow trout fishing. Marabou lures, Buzzers, Bugs, Hoppers and Emergers, to name but a few new fly designs, are now all seen in use alongside traditional patterns on England's lakes – changed days indeed.

It is frankly unfeasible to try and dissect the vast array of English fishing on offer (as with Scotland there are many excellent guidebooks already on the market) so instead I have selected but a few examples of what can be considered on-going cornerstones in English trout fishing. In other words the waters have deep historical roots and their operation in the twenty-first century is not drastically changed. These fishings I hope help show some of the quintessential essence of all things trouty in this country. Both are from the south of England but I would like to point out that the north has not been forgotten for it has already featured in the Scottish section of the River Tweed which rises in Scotland but ends up across the border in England. The first water featured is the rather unsung River Frome in Dorset, a classic chalkstream in the Test mould but far less reported and it has to be said much more realistically priced. It was here that some of the earliest experiments in dry fly angling for brown trout were done by G S Marryat, Halford's mentor and friend. The second is Blagdon Lake which was one of the earliest reservoirs to be opened up to the general public for angling and has since bred some exceptionally talented rainbow trout fishermen. Many of the lake skills first developed on Blagdon are now in universal use for rainbow trout across the UK. I feel it unfair to name specific examples of small commercially run stillwaters and there are literally thousands, however the methods previously mentioned for lake fishing are pretty universal. So let's press on…

River Frome

I selected this river as an English 'cornerstone' not because it is one of the best known, as you probably know a huge amount of material already exists on famous streams like the Test and Itchen, but because I wanted to highlight a river which essentially typifies a reasonably accessible chalkstream in southern England. First let me clarify this is the Dorset Frome and not other streams to the north. This river rises near Evershot in west Dorset and flows to the

Threading a cast on the Frome

east for around thirty-five miles past the towns of Dorchester and Wareham before meeting the sea at Poole harbour. Salmon and sea trout were at one time prolific on the Frome however in recent years catches of migratory species have declined in number. Brown trout are the main quarry for anglers, fortunately there does not seem to be any major incursion of rainbows into this river as yet. On some of the beats stocked browns have been introduced and these are marked with a blue dot. Anglers catching these can take a brace home if they wish but are asked to return any unmarked trout as these fish are capable of naturally reproducing in the wild.

The river has a wonderfully long history attached with links stretching back as far as King Henry VIII in the 1500s who granted the borough of Wareham together with its sporting and fishing rights to Catherine of Aragon. This is also 'Hardy country'. Legendary English writer and poet Thomas Hardy was born in Dorset in 1840 and amongst other settings used a considerable part of the Frome catchment area to form the backdrop for some of his famous novels including *Far from the Madding Crowd* and *Tess of the d'Urbevilles* both published in the latter 1800s. Angling connections include the legendary fly fisher G S Marryat who fished the Frome in the late 1800s and was a member of the Dorchester Fishing Club. As well as being an expert caster, Marryat was as an innovative fly tyer. The idea of upright split wings appears to have been his invention and it also seems probable he was one of the first anglers to try and imitate the mayfly nymph. It is almost certain Marryat would have been inspired to devise some of his first dry flies while fishing the Frome, patterns which Halford then went on to push into the forefront of English angling. It is sometimes said that had there been no Marryat there would have been no Halford. However though the latter tried to get Marryat credited for his help in collating his famous books on dry fly, Marryat insisted on remaining out of the limelight. Why such a great fisherman desired such anonymity is not clear but English fly fishing would be much the poorer without his contributions. The Frome also has links with the famous American based angler and conservationist Roderick Haig Brown who was born in Dorset in 1908. Haig Brown almost certainly would have fished the Frome in his formative years prior to moving to America where he wrote amongst other famous angling works the timeless *A River Never Sleeps*.

However it is not just the historical references which make this little river special. In many ways the Frome's wonderfully rich crystal clear waters strewn with waving ranaculus beds epitomise all that is best about an English chalkstream. The delightful surroundings of lush green fields, spreading trees, winding country lanes and tiny stone bridges complete a perfect country scene. No it's not a Hampshire Test with long sections of treeless carefully manicured lawns but in many ways this river is more true to the past with secretive brown trout lying hidden in the shady pools in much the same way as they did in the days of Marryat. In fact it's not difficult to imagine him with that great droopy cap pulled well down creeping along between the trees and now and again gliding out a perfect cast to catch an unwary fish. Today the casting of a line through at times dense patches of undergrowth will still test your skills to the limit and careful, delicate wading must be done upstream to try and tempt cautious trout. The clear cool fast flowing water provides a fabulously rich environment for the fish but it also means that the slightest showing of yourself on the skyline will send trout fleeing at speed. Outwith the mayfly hatch of May and June you have to fight for the fish here for they do not give themselves up easily.

The natural hatches on the Frome are on a par with any of the more famous chalkstreams with amongst others excellent Mayfly, Sedge including Grannom, Iron Blues, Black Gnats and Olives. Traditionally flies like the Houghton Ruby, small Sedge patterns, Black Gnat and Tup's Indispensable would be used but today many anglers favour tiny CDC dry fly patterns right down to about a size 22. As a confirmed long standing fisher of Scottish waters particularly lochs I fished Richard Slocock's Wrackleford

Flies for the Frome

beats on the River Frome one humid day in July in 2004. Compared to fishing my often peat stained waters I found this a wonderfully visual type of fishing. I could see big trout lying in the shady pools and cast upstream to a rise gamely trying to thread the fly line through dense undergrowth while at the same time avoiding spooking any leviathans skulking below. Being one to enjoy a real contest I actually found it great fun whizzing a cast between corridors of overhanging trees, huge rushes, strings of waving ranaculus and many a leafy bush; so different from Scotland's windswept heather moors but in truth I probably spooked more trout than I caught. In addition I had to use 2lb breaking strain leader and flies so small I could hardly see them. Gone too were my size 10 bushy beefy mouthfuls, instead a delicate selection of size 22 CDCs and olive nymphs took centre stage in the fly box. My 10ft rod was also far too over the top for this type of water (an 8ft rod would be sufficient) but I persevered. Fishing in miniature it might have been but it was all most enjoyable and a truly great day out.

Today the Frome is facing continuing and sustained threats from abstraction and a reducing water table. Enjoy it while you can and make your voice known especially with the powers that be who seem content to sit on their hands and do little to assist the long term conservation of one of England's last 'unchanged' chalkstreams.

Blagdon Lake

Blagdon Lake was once known as the Yeo Valley Reservoir and it began its illustrious history back in 1904 as one of earliest reservoirs opened up to the angling public. Interestingly

The wonderful Blagdon brown

despite being at the other end of the UK there is a strong Scottish connection with Blagdon as all the first managing staff employed were Scots. This was because the early Blagdon management wished the lake to have an almost 'Loch Leven' feel and expert staff were 'imported' to supervise the operation of the on site hatchery. Brown trout from Loch Leven were the first fish to be introduced into Blagdon and these were reared directly from native Leven brood stock. These brownies were of particularly high quality and in 1906 trout ova were successfully exported to the South Island of New Zealand where the eggs were hatched out and young trout planted out in the rivers. Thus Blagdon reared trout were the first strain of trout on the South Island.

Rainbow trout have also been matured at Blagdon right from the early 1900s and these fish together with browns and a few 'blue' trout are regularly stocked. The latter fish are an odd hybrid mix of browns and rainbows with a defined blue colour on their backs similar in nature to the Orrin Blues bred near Inverness. Stocking of the lake is largely done according to anglers' catch returns and both browns and rainbows are stocked pre season from the hatchery operating at the lakeside at Ubley. Running the hatchery is an extremely time consuming, labour intensive business. Brood stock are garnered from the rainbows and browns trying to run up the River Yeo at spawning time. These trout are then stripped and fertilised in the usual manner and a continual grading process begins to ensure only the best trout make it back to the lake. Supplementary mixed stock also has to be bought in to allow a sufficient growing on time for the hatchery fish yet at the same time allow plentiful stocking to meet the anglers' demands.

Nestling in the Mendip hills, Blagdon's 440 acres provide a super rich alkaline environment with greeny daphnia rich hue. In terms of feeding, this lake greatly resembles Scotland's or Ireland's shallow alkaline waters. The 'Blagdon Boil' is legendary and during this time tasty morsels the fish will feed on include lake/pond olives, ants, corixa, ants, damsel flies, snails, shrimp, caddis, daphnia, hawthorn flies and perch fry. The midge hatch is also critical on Blagdon and many anglers fish Buzzers and little else during their time there. Chironomid gulping continues throughout the season with claret, red, orange, black and green the top colours for midge imitations. The Blagdon Green Midge is renowned amongst English fly fishers and the importance of buzzers cannot be underestimated as is you're ability to fish them properly. Fishing can be carried out either from the boat (there are sixteen for hire) or off the bank. The long narrow shape of the lake with plenty of small bays and inlets makes for a splendid variety of trout holding areas. For a relatively large lake the depth is quite shallow averaging 14ft and 42ft at its deepest point at the dam.

The importance of Blagdon and its sister lake Chew in terms of developing reservoir angling techniques cannot be overstated. Eminent English angler Plunket Greene fished it with the equally eminent H T Sheringham back in 1912 and Greene remarks on the supreme fighting qualities of its brown trout especially during the evening rise. He preferred dry fly especially a Wickham's Fancy and found Blagdon night fishing quite hypnotic in its attractions. 'The silent pull in the darkness by the embankment at Blagdon is as potent a destroyer of conscience as a pull of wood-alcohol' – heady fishing indeed! During the 1930s well known local anglers Dr Bell and Paul Hill were hugely innovative in their imitative approach to fishing Blagdon. In the very early days angling was confined to attractor patterns in the large salmon fly mode and tandem patterns of traditional design. Gillies worked the boats and a large salmon fly was almost always the first choice to give to their eager clients. While Bell and Hill did not completely change the face of angling techniques which later became lure fishing they did develop imitative patterns like the Blagdon Buzzer and made anglers aware that there was more than just one way to skin the cat! Then in the 1980s with competition angling reaching new heights of popularity, Bristol anglers like Chris Ogborne and his colleagues helped reshape many of the tactics used on stillwaters. Buzzer fishing in particular came to prominence partly through the efforts of the Bristol anglers honing their fishing techniques on these lovely lakes. Like it or not, competitive fishing events held at Blagdon and Chew have been a powerful influence on how many anglers tackle lake fishing in the twenty-first century.

Bearing all this in mind I was lucky enough to visit Blagdon in its centenary year and experience what this famous lake had to offer first hand. Register of Experienced Fly Fishing Instructors and Guides (REFFIS) colleague Mike Gleave was an extremely helpful guide and an absolute font of local knowledge having worked for Bristol Water for forty plus years. Mike has spent many years managing and fishing this lake and our first stop was Butcombe Bay situated directly opposite Blagdon's wonderful Victorian fishing lodge complete with its dusty carvings of some of the biggest rainbows and browns to come from the lake in the 1920s. Despite the flat calm, some fish were sipping and rising and Mike advised a team of nymphs on 16ft fluorocarbon tippet with the three flies well spaced. 'Why fluorocarbon?' I asked suddenly feeling my trusted nylon was being made redundant. The answer was simple, fluoro sinks quickly through the water whereas nylon takes a deal longer.

Choice of fly was not entirely what I normally use either with skinny Black Buzzers and Diawl Bach variants (see Wales) the current top patterns for Blagdon at the time of my visit. I did sneak on the odd sparse Brora Ranger while Mike wasn't looking but sad to say, despite the old Scottish connections, the fish were having none of it. Having received a generous selection of Diawl Bachs to work with I set to the task. Fortunately Mike had the first throw as I was to discover Blagdon style is definitely not loch style. Forget fast retrieves and dibbling top droppers, this is a distant cast and a very slow twitched retrieve, so slow in fact the calm still air almost made for nodding off!

Mike Gleave at home on Blagdon

A few Blagdon specials

A lot of the fishing at Blagdon is done at anchor rather than on a drift, again an alien concept for a Scot used to loch style. The flies are cast and left to hang as dead insects sinking through the layers of water down towards the bottom. The wind puts a belly into the line as the flies fall and hardly any retrieve is required. Rainbows in particular take this type of fly presentation hard below the surface. Unfortunately for both the local expert and the naive visitor still trying to fish this way, fishing at anchor didn't prove productive off the north shore and instead we upped anchor and changed position to fish some southern bays.

Eventually a light ripple brought some relief from the incredibly flat water and a gentle drift was attempted. Almost immediately Mike was into fish and after a strong fight netted not a rainbow but a beautiful Blagdon reared brown trout which was carefully returned. A few drifts later I too captured a wonderful brown on the Diawl Bach but only after much chiding from Mike not to fish my flies fast; old habits die hard! If you want a challenge with plenty of history attached then this water is without doubt worth a visit. I must own up and say I achieved only modest success in what are classed as terrible conditions (there is actually a bag limit of eight trout per session) but if you want well managed, historic fishing in a peaceful Somerset environment this is the place.

SECTION 3

WALES

River Teifi

Chapter 11

Trout Fishing in Wales

The Trout of Wales

Geographically speaking this country has far more spate river than lake trout habitats. This effectively means the original trout populations colonising after the last Ice Age adopted a more roving migratory lifestyle with a high proportion of native Welsh trout developing sea going behaviour. Most of us already know that the sea trout is simply a brown trout which has adapted to feeding at sea for perhaps two or three years before returning to its natal stream to spawn. In Wales the opportunities for trout to assume the oceanic mantle are immense. True there are also high Welsh tarns and lakes with landlocked indigenous brown trout or a mix of browns and introduced rainbows the main quarry, but by and large the modern angler will usually visit Wales in search of its river dwelling migratory trout known locally as the much prized sewin.

Sewin weighing anything from a pound to perhaps 12lb or more are prolific in many Welsh rivers, even apparently tiny overgrown streams and these spanking silver trout happily coexist with both the smaller native browns and the Atlantic salmon. It is highly likely that given the close proximity of fish spawning redds in many Welsh rivers, a good number of the sewin will contain a percentage of salmon genes much akin to the trout of the River Tweed. This would account for their super strength and agility in fast flowing streams. Clear, fast flowing gravel 'freestone' rivers are a feature of the Welsh landscape and while sea trout and salmon grow big, the migratory native river brown trout tend to remain little never attaining much over a few ounces in weight.

Regarding Welsh trout in general it is interesting that the old Welsh name for a brown trout is 'brithyll' derived from the word 'brith' and this means the speckled one. This title is rather similar to the Scots word 'breac' which also means spotted or speckled. The origin of the Welsh term 'sewin' is a little more obscure. The earliest mention comes from writings of the 1500s which record 'samones', 'gyllynges' and 'suwynges'; salmon, grayling and sewin respectively. There is also the thought put forward by angling historian C B McCully that the term sewin might come from the Old English word 'sae-wynn' meaning sea-joy – a lovely but unfortunately non provable description. During the nineteenth century when it was fashionable to give trout different names and (wrongly) class them as separate species, other trout to be found in Wales included not only the sewin known then as *Salmo Cambricus* but also the darkly marked 'black finned trout' – *Salmo Nigripinnis* – which were caught in high mountain tarns. In addition there was the lesser known 'redfin' which was found in the River Wnion at Dolgellau (sometimes spelt Dolgelly) in NW Wales. The redfin was not to be confused with the 'torgoch' which was a red bellied char found in Lake Bodlyn near Llanberis in Caernarvonshire. Gallichan in 1903 gives an interesting account of how the redfin had intrigued Messrs Buckland, Cholmondeley Pennell and Calderwood, these gentlemen all being considered distinguished ichthyologists at that time. Gallichan notes the redfin was a small silvery trout with a blue tinge on its back, faint red spots and bright red caudal fin. He guesses

The much revered sewin

these were small sewin (sea trout), a reasonable enough assumption. However the great and good of that era thought differently and Gallichan mentions that Calderwood was intent on publishing findings concluding redfin to be a different species. Perhaps with the onset of the First World War this paper does not seem to have been published, probably just as well given that all trout are now classed as *Salmo trutta*.

Other unusual fish worth mentioning though not a trout as such is the now extremely rare gwyniad which is indeed a separate species related to the schelly in England and the powan of Loch Lomond in Scotland. The gwyniad looks like a silvery freshwater herring and was netted from Bala Lake in North Wales in considerable number to provide food during the nineteenth and early twentieth centuries. Gallichan writing in 1903 quaintly gives a description of the gwyniad saying that one authority had averred the flavour of this white fish to be 'so exquisitely delicate as to more than rival in flavour the lips of the fair maids of Bala'. Unfortunately the survival of the gwyniad is greatly in question today. Bala Lake has been considerably over fished by nets in the past and now has suffered from introductions of alien fish like ruffe which eat gwyniad eggs. Consequently the gwyniad is now a protected species and efforts have been made locally to re-establish a nursery population in another lake in order to stop the slow extinction of this uniquely secretive fish.

Both brown and sea trout have long been much revered in Wales sometimes to the point of assuming mystical and quasi-religious power. Legend has it that up until the early twentieth century trout were sometimes kept in holy wells where they were said to have some mystical healing powers. One of the most famous of these wells was at Llanberis in

Gwynedd. A newspaper report in 1896 noted the addition of two new trout to this well and that the fish would normally live for half a century. The appearance of one of the trout while an invalid was 'taking the waters' was said to mean instant health. While we might now think of this as a superstitious old wives' tales it must be remembered that trout like canaries in the coal mines, are great indicators of a pure water system and that there might have been that this old tradition was a rudimentary test as to whether the well water had become contaminated.

Stocking of Trout

The nineteenth century English trend of adding 'new blood' to waters whether or not the fish were needed did permeate into the more populated areas of Wales but given the considerable number of less visited, less polluted game fishing rivers, the practice of intensive restocking does not appear to have been seized upon with quite the fervour it was in England and parts of Scotland. Yes in Wales, trout stock additions have formed part of overall management policies particularly in the flourishing commercial lakes and reservoirs, but there seems to have been a more concerted emphasis on maintaining native migratory fish stocks. By and large the practice of adding in extra imported browns and rainbows into local water systems has been confined to stillwaters. Given the high quality of wild sea trout and salmon present in Welsh rivers the number of flowing waters seeing deliberate rainbow trout introductions are in the minority which has been good news for native game fish stocks.

This is not to say that stock enhancement does not take place on Welsh rivers and streams; modern angling pressures sometimes make it essential, however in most cases it is usually done by introducing sea trout fry and smolts from genetically pure native stock in line with local river management plans.

Environmental Change

Since the 1800s just as in England, waters nearest to the main centres of conurbation in Wales have seen a similar share of industrial pollution. Pressures on game fish waters have come from both heavy industry, copper and tin mining and agricultural practices and over time, losses of native fish stocks have undoubtedly occurred on various waters. Walter Gallichan also known as Geoffrey Mortimer, writing in *Fishing in Wales* in 1903 points out that a major cause of fish destruction was the modern system of field drainage over which at that time anglers and river authorities had no control. Further to that he also describes a river as being heavily polluted with sludge from a nearby copper mine. During the twentieth century the Welsh National Water Development Authority became responsible for the care and conservation of local waters, however Welsh rivers and lakes now all come under the Environmental Agency umbrella and as such are subject to the same legal constraints as in neighbouring England.

Despite concerns over the periodic swings in the numbers of sewin returning to different river systems in Wales perhaps caused through environmental change, the savage decline of sea trout already seen in Scotland and along parts of the Irish coastline has not happened here. Without doubt this can be attributed to the fact that the Welsh Assembly never really embraced promoting the fish farming industry in estuary waters (prime sea trout habitat) in quite the same way the Scottish Executive and Irish governments did. Today anglers in Wales can still enjoy tremendous game fish angling on a wide variety of rivers the length and breadth of the country together with superb stillwater brown and rainbow trout angling on the many small reservoirs and lakes which dot the countryside.

In Wales there is more of an emphasis on maintaining migratory fish stocks in rivers

Early Fishing Methods

Coracles

Wales is quite unique in respect of its early fishing methods for these were often carried out with the assistance of a hand crafted coracle. The coracle is a particularly ancient form of water transportation dating back to the sixth century AD if not a good deal earlier. These neat little craft were described in 1188 by one Gerallt Gymro as a small individual or two man oval-shaped boat made of willow 'almost round in shape and covered in skins'. At that time coracles were in common use both to fish from and to cross rivers and their employment continued until the latter half of the twentieth century. Fishermen would sit on a small wooden seat and paddle along the river by using a rudimentary wooden oar. Different rivers would have different shapes of coracle unique to their area and it was said that this may have helped distinguish local fishermen from interlopers.

For the working man using a rod and line from a coracle was initially a rare occurrence rather the fishermen would string nets between them to catch salmon and sea trout while the fish were swimming up river but also sometimes to take fish resident in lakes. These nets were initially woven from local materials like rushes rather akin to the Anglo Saxon nettle nets. The net which would be held across the flow of the river between two men seated in coracles, would be weighted with lead or similar on the base and have a cork neck. In this way the current would open the net out like a bag and unsuspecting fish would be trapped in its centre. Interestingly in the late nineteenth and early twentieth centuries the two man coracle was used for rod and line fishing by the leisured classes especially on bigger rivers like the

The unique Welsh coracle

Welsh Dee. The angler would have his attendant paddle the craft and keep it near to the best lies for salmon and trout while he would cast his fly. Effectively, skilled local coracle men could supplement their income by acting like a Scottish gillie for the wealthy rods visiting Wales.

Although the ordinary fly angler did use the coracle to fish various Welsh rivers, simply because of the craft's instability, one false move and you are tipped unceremoniously in the drink; on larger waters the coracle has never really proved serious competition to the traditional rowing boat. By the late twentieth century their use had all but died out, however given that coracles are a uniquely Welsh form of quirky water transportation they are still well worth a mention. Rather sadly, today the little crafts are mainly museum pieces occasionally given an airing for the benefit of tourists.

Chests and Baskets

From earliest times the rivers of Wales have quite literally teemed with game fish and throughout history salmon and sea trout have played an important part in the supply of food for local people. Right from when their culinary delights were first discovered, fish have been avidly consumed. Any surplus stocks were 'exported' to the English markets and the sale of salmon and sea trout was a thriving business providing vital income for the vendors. From Roman times ingenious systems were devised to trap migrating fish as they made their way back from the sea and up into their natal streams. The basic methods of doing this were by net, baskets or chests. Akin to their early fellow fishermen in Scotland and England, Welsh fishers used wide necked triangular wicker baskets suspended under waterfalls into which the salmon would fall as it tried to leap upstream. Once caught in the narrow base of the basket it was impossible for the fish to leap out again.

In addition to using baskets to catch fish, the use of chests sunk into the river and held in place by rocks and walls was also widespread. Weirs like impenetrable fences would be placed across the water flow to divert fish, in Scotland these were known as cruives. These would often be made of stout willow or hazel designed to form narrow channels in the stream through which the migrating fish would be forced to travel. Once in the channel the fish would begin nosing upstream only to find themselves trapped inside the sunken trap. These chests were cleverly devised to have wooden planks or doors which opened sufficiently to let the fish pass through but then the force of the current would quickly force the door shut behind the fish allowing no means of escape. Sometimes the fishermen would use long poles to physically drive any salmon hiding in the corners of pools into the waiting chest. Though salmon was the main quarry many larger sea trout would be ensnared by this means.

Other Fishing Methods

As in all other UK countries a fair number of Welsh fishermen were skilled in using less than savoury not to say dubious fishing techniques equated more with poaching than the gentle art. These methods varied from cross lining when a long line of baited hooks or flies strung out from the shore or run between two coracles, to otter boarding (see also Scotland) where a plank of wood would be floated out with a line with baited hooks or flies attached. Night lines also known as the 'gwest' or the 'tant' would also be set and these were also effective in producing fish. Nineteenth century Welsh folklore historian and angler Elis o'r Nant (also known as Ellis Pierce) tells of making woven horsehair lines from mountain ponies' tails on which baited hooks would be fastened. The horsehair line would be attached to a specially made wooden peg or stake and left out overnight to catch fish. In Scotland this is known as a set line.

Other ugly methods involved gaffing fish (usually salmon) with harpoons, tridents and big hooks, also snaring the fish with loop snares fashioned like the modern salmon tailer or foul hooking big fish stuck in low water pools, a technique also referred to as 'snatching'. Occasionally explosives were used especially by mining or quarry men who had first hand knowledge of how to best employ them. All these fishing methods are now illegal in Wales and throughout the UK and carry heavy fines which, given the concern across the UK nationally over the general decline in game fish species, is just as well.

Developing Rod and Line Angling

Through the nineteenth and first half of the twentieth century fishing methods were somewhat divided according to social class with the local working man employing an inexpensive home produced rod to bring in his catch, while the fishing gentry often fly fished with expensive rods and other angling paraphernalia imported from tackle dealers based in England and Scotland. Even if locals did fly fish, many had to make do with local materials to make their equipment. Elis o'r Nant records in his youth using hazlewood cut from local forests to fashion his fishing rod. Interestingly he noted that sometimes they made rods in two or three pieces and that there was a local unwritten law which necessitated cutting one rod section from the bottom of the hill, one from the middle and one from the top of the hill. He indicated that he didn't really know the reason as to why this was done rather he said 'this was the way we had been taught; we did not know why.' Today we know that wood from the lower slopes is older and stiffer and suited to making the butt of a rod while wood from the upper slopes would be more pliable. The local Welsh rod maker would therefore benefit from these features making a rod which had a reasonable flexing action rather than one which was ramrod stiff. Further accounts of local materials being used for fishing tackle come from Hugh Derfel Hughes who in 1866 recounts that 'the old people' made their fishing rods from dried hazlewood to which they would attach tapered horsehair lines sometimes with a gut cast and put on an artificial fly in order to tempt trout. Interestingly he makes reference to attaching 'a Limerick hook (a hook of Irish origin) carefully concealed with a fly' on the main leader. Could this perhaps be a copy of W C Stewart's tandem hook flies or indeed the forerunner of Falkus's two hook Secret Weapons so popular now in sewin fishing?

As with the rest of the UK it was during the nineteenth century that sporting rod and line fishing really began to grow in popularity in Wales. Principal exponents of the gentle art came from the upper echelons of society with wealthy merchants and industrial barons buying up fishing rights on various rivers to make game fishing an integral and exclusive part of their leisure pursuits. The quality of sport enjoyed in those early days was beyond the superlative. During the 1800s even on the lesser known smaller rivers, it was not uncommon for anglers to catch seventy plus small trout (probably a mix of browns, immature sewin and salmon parr) in one day. These numbers equate with the huge catches being made on the Scottish Tweed by Stewart and company at roughly the same time. Throughout the 1900s similar tales of hefty catches abound notably from the river Teifi and the lake of Tal-y-llyn also abound with dozens upon dozens of heavy trout and sewin being taken in a single day; according to Lynn Hughes writing in Moc Morgan's *Flies of Wales* one noted angler Thomas Medwin apparently had the nerve to complain of aching shoulders after carrying back a day's catch of seventy-two trout from the Teifi!

To some extent the gentry's exploitation of game fish from largely untouched Welsh streams caused a degree of tension amongst local fishermen who believed they had a long held birth right to enjoy the bounty of the river without payment or restriction, especially when native fish were seen as an important source of food rather than a rich man's plaything. During the 1800s this apparent antipathy between the common man on the one hand and the gentry on the other was further exacerbated when wealthy 'foreigners' bought up many river fishing rights and imported their own bailiffs to keep their new acquisitions for their exclusive use. Poaching became an often necessary means of supplying a meal on the table. However from the late nineteenth and into mid twentieth centuries the romantic image of the old poacher taking 'one for the pot' was increasingly replaced by organised peripatetic gangs of thugs intent on stripping rivers bare of their fish and then selling them on the black market for financial gain. Walter Gallichan writing in *Fishing in Wales* in 1903 bemoans the fact that concerted poaching was rife in Wales stating 'I will freely concede that Welsh salmon and trout might be, and indeed should be, very much better than it is. There is perhaps, more ruthless poaching all year round in Wales than in any other part of Britain'. He also pointed out that poaching was at that time romanticised by many, court fines were paltry and that few locals or magistrates were willing to view poaching as a form of robbing one's neighbours preferring instead to dismiss it as a far lesser crime.

It should be noted that despite knowledge of fly fishing becoming established during the blossoming sport fishing era of the nineteenth and twentieth centuries, many local anglers

Fishing methods are used according to the river conditions with many rivers allowing both fly and spinner

preferred bait fishing or more particularly fishing with the worm. Some were and indeed still are highly skilled with the technique of trotting worms down on a river. There is a lovely description of one twentieth century worm fishing expert Owen Roberts of the Ffestiniog area which appears in the booklet *Traditional Fishing in Wales* by Emrys Evans. It runs

> Addolwr afon ddulwyd
> A'I hyder llawn mewn 'dwr llyd'.

This translates beautifully to mean:

> One who worshipped a dark grey river
> And had total confidence in the 'grey waters'.

A wonderfully lyrical description of a worm fisher if ever there was one!

Today rod and line fishing in Wales is a happy democratic mix of worm, spinner and fly. These methods are now used largely according to water height and colour rather than because of any social nuance and that is just the way it should be.

Chapter 12

WELSH FISHING SKILLS

River Fishing

Broadly speaking the rivers of Wales differ in two ways from the spring fed chalkstreams of the neighbouring English shires. Firstly a good number of Welsh waters are rocky spate streams, rising and falling according to rainfall and/or snow melt. They range from gin clear in low water to peat stained and silt coloured when in high flood. Most are fast flowing waters demanding a high degree of stealth and accuracy in fly casting. Water quality can vary from hour to hour and the angler really needs to be up on his or her watercraft adapting tactics to suit the local conditions. While the feeding for trout is reasonable it does not quite match the headiness of the rich chalkstream habitats and this too will influence how you fish there.

Secondly, Welsh rivers have a much higher presence of migratory fish within their systems than in England and this demands a somewhat different approach when fishing. The prominent presence of the super cautious sewin along with salmon and brown trout makes for a particularly demanding challenge. It also means using sewin flies which are a little different from the traditional straightforward wet or dry patterns. The environment and the fish lurking within therefore set the tone of how you must fish in Wales, adapting techniques both to local habitats and fish species.

Wet Fly and Nymph for River Trout

If you look at both old and modern writings on Welsh fishing for trout it quickly becomes obvious that the wet and dry fly techniques used on Welsh rivers do not differ that much from English and Scottish tactics devised specifically to fish fast flowing spate rivers. Broadly speaking traditional Welsh river fly fishing is an interesting mix of inherent local skills merged with imported techniques brought to the country from England and to a certain extent Scotland. The Welsh angler seems to have had a canny knack of taking the best of other river skills and making them their own. In fact given the nature of the terrain and the virtual absence of lush mayfly hatches so obsessively revered by the anglers of the southern English shires, the river angling styles of Wales bear a significantly close resemblance to north country sunk fly tactics.

It would also appear that initially, early trout fly fishing tactics did not appear to make a clear distinction between fishing for sewin and brown trout angling, this was to happen later. By and large, fly tactics for river trout have developed around fishing time honoured wet flies either up and across or swinging them gently across and down the river. These methods are of course respectively akin to the northern England and Scottish river trout angling traditions and it's also interesting that in both river and lake fishing, teams of flies were often employed. According to G A Hansard writing in 1834 flies were sometimes tied on as droppers, indeed he refers to the Drop Fly which was apparently tied on the horsehair line by the ingenious means of a pig's bristle. As the bristle from a pig's snout is composed of clear stiff material this must

Wet fly on the Nevern (photo by N. Prichard)

have made one heck of a stand out dropper! The book the *Anglers' Handbook* written in the late 1800s also refers to sparse black wet flies as being particularly productive when fished Scottish fashion as multiple flies on a cast (leader) placed about 12 inches apart. The flies were apparently fished upstream akin to Scots doyen W C Stewart's tactics of the 1840s.

Long established favoured wet fly river patterns have normally tended to be tied sparse being made to imitate local natural insects like the stonefly, oak fly, sedges, beetles and olives. The Welsh fly tyers followed the sparse English and Scottish wet fly edict that flies should be tied sparse and skinny to allow 'good entry' into the water thus fishing at the correct depth without drag. For many years fly anglers contented themselves with a mix of traditional old local favourites and nationally known British patterns. Thus long established wet flies like, to name but a small number, the February Red, March Brown, Olive Quill, Black Pennell and Black Gnat sizes 12 to 16 would be fished alongside specially tied local patterns like the Black and Silver – a super sewin and brown trout fly reminiscent of a Zulu without the red tag; the Blue Hen a sparse wispy nymph like fly; the Usk Purple a representation of the iron blue nymph; the Cob, an imitation of the March Brown; the Orl a Welsh version of the traditional Alder Fly and so on.

Regarding nymphs it is interesting that the oldest Welsh designed trout patterns are vaguely similar to the north country sparse nymph type patterns, delicate quick sinking and imitative in style rather than simply general attractors. During the latter half of the twentieth century more modern nymph patterns were 'imported' and added to the overall repertoire notably those popular nymphs like the Pheasant Tail and the Hare's Ear. From the 1990s on many

133

weighted nymph variants, the so called Bugs and Heavy Nymphs, have appeared on the British and European fly tying scene and these have been incorporated into Welsh river angling proving highly popular on local fast flowing streams.

Dry Fly on Welsh Rivers

As we have already seen in the chapters on English dry fly the latter half of the nineteenth century saw an explosion in popularity in angling with the floating fly. The question now arises whether the Welsh river angler took dry fly to his heart in quite the same way as his English neighbours. Undoubtedly dry fly was brought to Wales by English visiting anglers who would employ the nouveau floating fashion while fishing private stretches of river however it appears that it took a good deal longer for the dry fly to be truly absorbed into Welsh river fishing culture. Again the fact that migratory trout were often the target coupled with the need to search deep pools with a sunk fly appears to have dictated the widespread use of the wet fly over the dry. There is also a train of thought that to some extent the Welsh were already using a version of floating flies as several of the well hackled local patterns must have sat high on the water surface until they eventually sank. Gallichan in 1903 describes various hackled non winged flies as effective on the River Conway notably what he calls the Sooty Hackle with black bushy hackle and dull orange body. Effectively these would float in fast water and though we have no way of proving it, many trout must have been caught while the fly was still 'dry'.

Happily, despite the initial hesitancy in accepting apparently new fangled English ideas (both the Scots and the Welsh seemed to share this cautious approach), dry fly is now a readily accepted technique for both browns and sewin. As in other areas of the UK a number of essentially wet flies have over the years been converted into dry versions. A good example of this is Dai's Alder. Dai Lewis was a famous twentieth century river Teifi angler renowned for his fly tying skill. Basically this pattern is a neat non winged version of the English Alder fly which was remade as a floater. Other normally wet patterns redone to form Welsh dry flies included the Coachman (Hackled), the Badger, Red Tag and the March Brown. In addition there are some supremely useful Welsh dries tied by local anglers. Dai Lewis made the Paragon to imitate sedges and given the fly's brown wispy appearance it would undoubtedly catch trout anywhere in the UK. Another highly successful local dry fly is the Welshman's Button tied by well respected angler Tom Tom of mid Wales probably made to represent a beetle. Again the use of peacock herl for the body and subtle mixing of red and black game hackles for the head hackle gives this fly definite fish attractiveness and I'm certain this fly would be successful anywhere in the UK.

Although the dry fly has secured a place in Welsh river trout angling especially when cast upstream in low water conditions it has never seen the obsessive use that it did across in the shires of southern England. This is probably due to the nature of the Welsh spate stream which calls for much more switching of tactics according to water height. Thus dry fly can have its day when great delicacy is called for on clear pools where brown and/or migratory trout are resting but is less used during a high coloured spate when fish are travelling fast through the river system.

Specialist Fishing for Sewin

It is important to remember that real specialism in Welsh river sea trout angling has only come comparatively recently. Before the 1960s fly fishing for sewin was done by using an eclectic mix of salmon sunk line tactics and/or traditional wet fly trout fishing. Flies of the

Many Welsh sewin anglers have embraced the Falkus doctrine

salmon mould were in large sizes 4 to 8 and Silver Doctor, Black Doctor and Silver Charm were perennial favourites. These would normally be fished using the essentially Scottish technique of across and down on a sunk line. Trout wet flies in common use in the first half of the twentieth century were highy traditional wets: Pennells, Butcher, Mallard and Claret, Alexandra, Badgers and Zulus used in teams of two, three or four employed in the up and across or across and down method in very similar fashion to the traditional wet fly river trout tactics used by Scottish and Irish anglers in that same period.

Today a much expanded range of flies and ploys are in use for sewin, largely inspired by English angler Hugh Falkus who wrote a seminal tome *Sea Trout Fishing* in the 1960s with a revised expanded edition in 1975. The theories Falkus propounded allowed Welsh sewin fishing to develop and grow. To some extent the way had been paved for Falkus by a noted Welsh angler F W Holiday who had written *River Fishing for Sea Trout* in 1960. Holiday expounded the use of the subsurface lure on a sunk line for night fishing and also advocated tube flies and Waddingtons to catch sewin. These were fairly innovative theories in the 60s and Falkus took them even further. Falkus may have fished mainly on the Border Esk but the tactics he developed there are perfect for sewin fishing. He advocated a highly systematic approach to night fishing for sea trout using a selection of flies like Medicines, Surface lures, Sunk lures and Secret Weapons and devised a strategy for using these flies in that order through the hours from dusk to dawn. Put very simply, in the first half of the night Falkus advocated fishing the flies high and fast on a floating line then after midnight/1am the fly should be fished deep and slow using a sunk line. For daylight angling Falkus advocated using similar wet flies and lures but really only when the water is high and slightly coloured.

Welsh sewin anglers embraced the Falkus doctrine and were and still are highly successful with it. There are perhaps two fundamental reasons why the Englishman's sea trout tactics have done so well in Wales. The first is the easy translation of techniques used on the fast flowing Border Esk where Falkus developed and devised his trade to the clear spate rivers of Wales. The second reason is that most of the early twentieth century recording of sea trout skills prior to Falkus had been by Scots like Bridgett, Henzell and Mottram all of whom were specialist loch anglers. Though some of the old masters' loch skills could be adapted to a Welsh river when Falkus came along it was much easier to adopt his ideas. You will see his concepts much in use today sitting happily alongside the modern ethos of sewin angling. In this respect one of the most influential has been Welsh angler, author and broadcaster Moc Morgan who wrote *Successful Sea Trout Angling* with Graeme Harris in 1989. This hugely comprehensive book, based largely on Moc's experiences of sewin angling in West Wales notably on the River Teifi, builds on Falkus's vision exploring a wide range of techniques for sea trout.

Modern Sewin River Techniques

Today's fishing for sewin can generally be divided up into daytime fishing and angling at night. Thankfully in Wales the illusion that sea trout can never be caught in daylight is understood for what it is – a myth. Local sewin anglers tend to lay much more store on following the conditions: water height, colour and speed of flow than they do simply blindly adhering to past dogma and doctrine. There follows a very basic description of the unique skills required to catch the secretive silver sewin:

Sewin by day

Fishing in daylight can be done providing the water is high and slightly coloured so the sewin remain unaware of the angler's presence. Sewin are such cautious easily spooked fish you need the conditions to be just right. The day after heavy rain when the river is full and just beginning to fall is considered the best for day time angling with wet flies like Secret Weapons or similar always a popular choice. An intermediate or sinking line is used to keep the fly swimming at reasonable speed in fast water. Floating lines in daylight are a bit of a non-starter when the river is high; the fly simply does not stay in the water long enough. The wet fly is usually worked across and down the pool with particular attention being paid to the slacker water of the tail of the pool where the sewin might be pausing and preparing to ascend further upriver. When the spate has receded and the water cleared, sewin can still be caught if the day is dull and windy and the angler pays attention to the riffled rather than the slack water. Floating lines and dry fly (Olive patterns, Wickhams, etc) or small traditional wet flies like Pennell or Mallard and Claret fished upstream can still take fish but the angler must be super careful to hide his presence and present his fly with delicacy. For this reason many will wait until nightfall.

Night Sewin

Fishing for sewin in the hours of darkness is normally undertaken when the river is at a normal to low height. It is often a huge challenge and to be successful you need to reconnoitre in advance the pools you are going to fish. The absolute key to doing well in this weird and

Sewin in the dark! (photo by N. Prichard)

wonderful branch of trout fishing is doing your river homework well in advance. You need to know where the fish are likely to be, how you are going to cast to them without snagging flies, how to get in and out of the river without frightening the fish and also where you are going to net your catch. When you are stumbling about in pitch darkness the need for advance preparation will become patently obvious, believe me!

Fishing methods need to be used according to the conditions. Traditional wet fly or Secret Weapons fished across and down are effective in normal to high water bearing in mind the big water big fly idiom, while Falkus's floating fat bodied Wake flies are used on dark nights with little or no moonlight though to some extent these have been replaced by more modern flies like Muddler Minnows. A big dry fly upstream can be productive on moonlit nights when you can just about make out the shape of the fly. The Falkus idea of using sunk fly late into the night when the black is going to give way to the first grey light of another day is still used worked on intermediate or sinking line. Basically you need to be flexible with your tactics and go very much with the flow.

Modern Sewin Flies

Sewin flies did not exist during the nineteenth and early twentieth centuries. During that period sewin were caught almost by accident on salmon flies or fished for with big trout flies like the Zulu, Alexandra, Peter Ross or Dunkeld. However today we see a far wider range of patterns used these being devised to take into account whether it is to be fished in daylight or darkness and whether the river is high or low. In his book *Flies of Wales* Moc Morgan points out day fishing in normal to low water for sewin may require smaller flies of dull hue like the

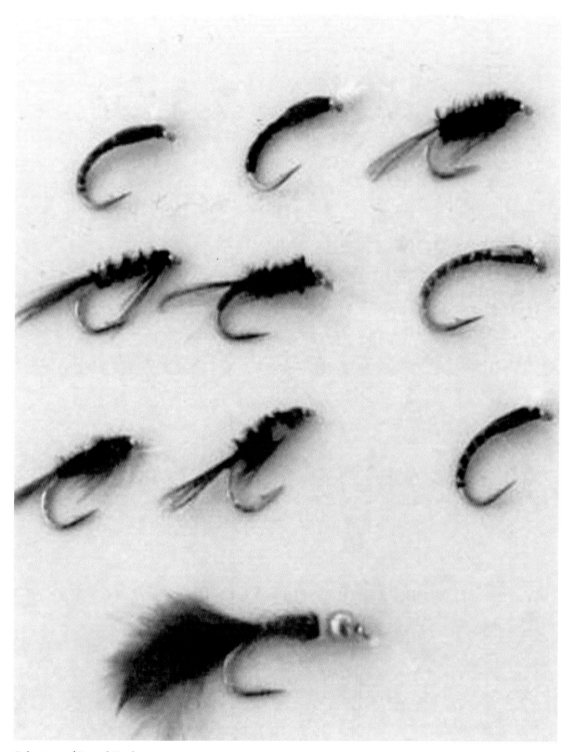

Selection of Diawl Bachs

Brown and Yellow Mole popular on the Towy while high coloured waters need larger silver bodied patterns often with a blue hackle like the Blue Black amd Silver (a variation of the ever successful Teal Blue and Silver) widely used on the Conway and the Teifi. If fishing at night Moc advises larger colourful patterns like the Allrounder or bigger flies with silver bodies constructed with hair wing on tandem hooks or tubes much akin to Falkus's Secret Weapons and Medicine flies. He also mentions that in 1996 Welsh sewin anglers had taken to using these patterns in bigger sizes making the flies not only on traditional single or tandem hooks but also employing Tubes, Trebles, Terrors and Waddingtons which shows that far from standing still the sport continues to evolve and grow.

Welsh Lake Fishing

While there are some excellent historically famous trout lakes notably Vyrnwy, Talyllyn and Llyn Brenig along with a proliferation of small mixed fish or rainbow fisheries it has to be said that all the techniques applied in Wales for stillwater fishing do not differ that much from the skills covered in lake/lough and loch fishing. That is not to say the Welsh have not pioneered stillwater techniques because they have devised some supremely good flies however there is not a great deal of difference between tactics used on Welsh lakes and tarns and those used elsewhere in the UK. Traditional wet fly, modern lures, dry fly and nymph angling techniques all sit happily together here and these are well covered in the Scottish and English lake/loch fishing sections.

Popular Modern Lake Patterns

The most successful stillwater patterns now used universally across the length of Britain are the Diawl Bach, the Coch Y Bondhu (also spelt Coch-a-bon-ddu) and the Haul a Gwynt. The Diawl Bach (Welsh for little devil) is now one of the most successful countrywide reservoir wet flies. Though it appears to have been tied to represent a dull coloured nymph form of perhaps a midge or an olive, it is now universally accepted for buzzer fishing and has a string of variants in different colours and tyings including 'anorexic' style see also England/Blagdon lake page 116. Fished slowly in teams on a dead drift it is hugely efficient in catching rainbows and brown trout of all sizes. The nineteenth century Coch Y Bondhu is of much more traditional mould, well palmered and every bit a fly lending itself to traditional loch style as the top dropper of a team of flies. In fact it is at home wherever there is a big sheet of water and rainbows and browns readily accept it. The fly was originally tied to represent a type of beetle with reddish brown body and red/black legs and was used as much in rivers as in lakes. During the 1980s however the Coch like the Diawl Bach took on a definite reservoir association proving highly successful in competition fishing. The Haul a Gwynt (sun and wind), which looks a bit like the Scottish fly the Kate McLaren, is another of the traditional mould and is extremely effective tripped along on a wave as the top dropper of a three fly cast.

Though the smaller range of Welsh lake flies cannot match the many thousands made for Scotland and Ireland, those patterns which have become well known have gained the distinction of being highly successful anywhere in the UK and they deserve great credit.

Chapter 13

CORNERSTONES OF WELSH TROUT ANGLING

I t must be made clear that Welsh trout fishing is no little sister to English, Scottish or Irish angling. In some respects it is quite unique for no other UK country sees quite the concentrated nocturnal fishing effort that goes on in Wales! Yes there has been a steady adoption and absorption of brown and rainbow trout skills from its bedfellows, but the sea trout angling techniques remain in a class of their own. Welsh anglers are passionate about their sewin angling and more than willing to share their tactics with visiting anglers. This is important for such is the range of excellent river and lake fishing it is difficult to know even where to begin. Rivers like the Towy, Teifi, Conwy, Taf, Cleddau, Cothi, Usk, Dee, Dovey and Dwyfor to name but a few are all famed for sewin angling and lakes like Vyrnwy and Talyllyn have provided great inland fishing for around a century or so.

The choice of Welsh waters which could illustrate its cornerstone angling is therefore immense. In the end it was decided to plump for waters famous for top quality sewin fishing as this is for what the country is most famed. In doing so I have selected one comparatively unknown hidden gem the River Nevern, so well run by its local anglers, and the esteemed well recognised Rivers Towy and Teifi, particularly the latter river where the Llandysul and Teifi Trout Association has achieved great things in acquiring and managing long stretches of the river for the benefit of local and visiting anglers.

Nevern Nirvana

Picture this for a moment. A beautiful gin clear stream where the glides are fast and the tree-shaded pools can positively heave with wonderful game fish fresh from the sea. Imagine this river having a bag limit for both visitors and local anglers of two salmon and four sea trout per day, not only that but given the right conditions the daily allowance is quite within the realms of possibility rather than vague fantasy figures. Equally think about a stream that's fly, bait or spinning, a place where you can freely choose your method according to the water height. Ponder on a well managed water democratically run by local anglers where daily tickets do not vary in price and you can fish seven days a week all season on about six miles of club owned or leased water. Not only that but even if you live in the next parish or in the next county for that matter, you are welcome to join the local angling association to fish for trout, sewin and salmon for the same price as the nearby residents, so different from a considerable number of Scottish rivers.

To find this Nirvana, take yourself off to Pembrokeshire in south-west Wales and fish the River Nevern. This little meandering stream is for its small size now considered one of the most productive spate rivers in Wales. Its source lies in the Bryn Berian hills and it empties into the wide sandy estuary at Cardigan Bay. The Nevern Angling Association own or lease around six miles of this lovely river where sewin up to 5 or 6lb mingle with small browns and

Nevern Nirvana

top quality salmon in the 10lb range. It must be said that the local angling club management has benefited the river enormously. With its careful genetically pure stocking plans, bank maintenance programmes and controlled season which closes the Upper Nevern in late September to allow fish safe access to spawning, the Nevern is an excellent example of what can be achieved to benefit wild game fish if anglers work harmoniously together. In fact this management structure is the envy of many similar organisations in the UK.

I was lucky enough to fish the Nevern during a rainy week in early September, one when all the different conditions that can occur on a spate river quite literally flashed before my eyes. Well known Welsh ladies' internationalist Nica Prichard who has fished on the Nevern for many years, volunteered to be my guide on this lovely winding stream. On reflection I can safely say it was the best quality fishing I had during 2004. Rarely have I enjoyed such action-packed angling in what amounted to only three or four days of fishing. The object of the exercise was to learn more about the habits of the sewin (Welsh sea trout) and how to catch them. Nica had issued stern warnings of having to fish all night in order to stand a chance of hooking a sea trout. Given the dense undergrowth that surrounds the Nevern this was one prospect I admit I did not greatly relish. When I arrived the river was racing down in full spate and the water appeared disappointingly clouded with silt and leaf litter. However my apprehension about these conditions was quickly dismissed when I discovered this meant we could fish during the day rather than at night as, in such high water, the sewin simply cannot see you. Falling over fences, negotiating 10ft high walls, slithering down banks and stumbling through fields was bad enough in daylight. Welsh sewin fishing I quickly learned has more than a touch of the mountain goat to it!

Nica kindly lent me a suitable sewin outfit. Light 9ft 6in rod, a Cortland Blue line (a slow sink intermediate), 8lb nylon and some neat self tied flies derived from Hugh Falkus's Secret Weapons. These patterns are basically old favourites like the Teal Blue and Silver and similar made more lethal with the addition of a small treble hook in tandem. Local anglers swear by these as they believe it largely stops the frustration of sewin just nipping the fly and making off without taking hold. Thus armed I was ready. Our first full day saw one salmon landed, one lost, several sewin taken mainly by spinning and some small native brown trout returned all in the space of around five hours. Not I have to say to my rod, I was too busy taking it all in and mastering how to thread the fly line between the Nevern's thick tree cover. At one point I thought I was setting new records for impaling flies in oak branches but Nica assured me many have gone before doing exactly the same thing.

Day two saw the river still coloured but dropping very slightly, optimism was in the air. Locals were busy spinning and worming but I stuck with fly mainly because my skills with a spinning rod largely match my tree and wall climbing abilities. There is a half hour rule for each pool on the Nevern and having watched an expert local thoroughly spin out the water with a huge Rappala only five minutes before I started, a little seed of Scots doubt was creeping in. Silly me as when the second across and down cast into this pool swung round to reach the pool's tail under an overhanging tree, a sudden solid contact was made. My first

A sewin at last! (photo by N. Prichard)

Welsh sewin may have only been a pound or so but it was a wonderfully athletic fish and made a fantastic evening meal. Nica urged me to keep fishing as where there is one there will be more and another couple of casts saw a much heavier fish seize the same Secret Weapon fly. This time there were no leaps and crashes just a heavy thumping on the end of the line. 'It feels like a salmon' I called to Nica who, having just got back up the bank again from netting the sewin, rapidly turned and slithered down again net at the ready. Anxious moments followed as the fish jarred on the well bent little rod below my uncomfortably high stance. I caught sight of its shining flank in a flash of sunlight. This was no sewin it was indeed a salmon and a fresh one at that, about 8 to 10lb. 'Champagne tonight if we get this on the bank' I squeaked breathlessly. Silly fool for with that utterance a determined racing charge upstream to my left began. In my over excitement I completely forgot all the rules about playing big fish on small rods in fast water and failed miserably to spot the bramble bush between me and the angry salmon. There was an almighty thudding swirl below, a ping and the great fish and I parted company forever.

Recovery from this albeit welcome shock took some time but my third and last day provided contact with two more sewin one of which was over 2lb again hooked on the Secret Weapon. Returning home via Cardiff and Edinburgh I could hardly believe what I had just experienced. Frankly this type of river fishing is a breath of fresh air when compared with some of my over priced northern rivers. Welsh fishing is impressively democratic, very much for all comers and demands considerable skill both with fly and spinning rod. Kings and commoners are treated as one, money does not necessarily buy you better fishing here and that is just how it should be.

Teifi and Towy Triumph

Even though catches have declined somewhat in recent years, the meandering Towy (also known as Tywi) in west Wales has long been associated with some of the best sea trout fishing in Britain. Anglers come from all over Europe to try for the big fast growing Towy sewin which can reach over 15lb with a conservative average weight of 3lb plus being the expected norm. In fact past records here indicate sewin as the dominant game fish with a recent ten year average declared rod catch at five thousand sewin compared with eight hundred salmon for the same period and that figure does not include the good sized resident brownies that inhabit the main sections of the river. With seventy-five miles of exciting fishing running from Llandeilo below the Brecon Beacons south-west down through the town of Carmarthen to the sea, the River Towy remains at the pinnacle of Welsh sea trouting but hard on its heels now is the Teifi.

The Teifi is a slightly smaller faster flowing stream than the Towy rising in the ancient Cambrian hills, running west down to Tregaron Bog and then meandering across a wide coastal plain to tip its waters into the sea at Cardigan Bay, west Wales. The sewin here though a little smaller than those of the Towy are equally prolific with catches growing in stature over the last twenty years or so. In addition some excellent brown trout are caught in this enigmatic rural water. Angling for salmon, sewin and brown trout takes place over around fifty miles or so of largely club owned or club leased waters. The principal beats centre on the Teifi Trout Association waters at Newcastle Emlyn, the Llandysul Angling Association stretch from just below Llandysul village up to the beats above Lampeter and the Cymdeithas Pysgota Tregaron Angling Association beats on the upper river valley. Great advances in what could be termed democratic angling have been made on the Teifi with forward thinking associations buying up fishing rights along the river as and when they have become available. This has opened up essentially private water and allowed local and visiting anglers to enjoy the river to the full. In addition local fishing groups have taken a keen interest in on-going fish conservation and river restoration projects which have benefited native fish stocks greatly.

In late 2004 I was lucky enough to visit one of the most delightful sewin and salmon angling areas of the Teifi which comes under the auspices of the Llandysul Angling Association. Esteemed chairman of this hard working group fellow Swan Hill author Pat O'Reilly gave his customary wise council and experienced local angler David Prichard led the way on a lovely streamy sewin-rich beat near the little village of Llandysul. For fly fishing (bait and spinning are allowed on certain beats) normal tactics for Teifi sewin centre on night fishing using a 10ft 6in rod, 8lb nylon, AFTM 7 floating, intermediate or sinking line and traditional flies like the Alexandra, Butcher, Teal Blue and Silver or Secret Weapons. Flies should be tried according to water height, big fly big water, little fly little water and the norm for night angling is to fish across and down the pools paying particular attention to areas under overhanging trees and the tails of the pools. If the pool is deep then a big wet fly cast upstream and allowed to come back on the fish can sometimes produce the goods. As always with sewin angling a considerable degree of experimentation not to say perseverance is required.

The Towy in flood

A cast in the Teifi

Given that the beautifully rural Teifi was high after a flood of rain, daylight angling for sewin was the choice and again the bigger flies like the Secret Weapon and the local fly the Teifi Terror were put to good use on a Cortland Blue slow sink line. Sadly although determined effort was made and although we saw salmon caught by fellow anglers spinning in the big water, the sewin on this occasion ignored our rods so instead I took time out to learn more of this prolific river's brown trout angling. Historically the Teifi has been a tremendous brown trout river especially in its upper reaches with considerable opportunities for dry fly, wet and nymph angling. Important local hatches include Mayfly, Hawthorn, March Browns, Caperer, Grannom and Blue Winged Olive. In May and June local anglers favour using the dry fly cast upstream; Rough Olive, Grey Wulff and G and H Sedge size 12 to 16 are popular choices to use on floating line with a normal water height when the trout are showing well. Sadly in the 1990s the brown trout stocks went into an unexpected cycle of decline both in size and general numbers caught, however all credit to the Llandysul Angling Assocation for instigating sound conservation measures and initiating habitat improvement for juvenile trout. Their actions have led to a steady improvement in brown trout stocks.

Though the Welsh names for the beats on this luscious river are often unpronounceable to outsiders, being as much a challenge to fathom as the mysteries of the sewin, the Teifi is a Welsh river to revere and revisit. I must return and do better justice to it....

SECTION 4

IRELAND

Chapter 14

THE TROUT OF IRELAND

Not without good reason will the prospect of going fishing for Ireland's wonderfully diverse trout set the dedicated angler's pulse racing. The country is quite simply a game fisher's paradise laced with rivers and studded with loughs all with their own enigmatic character. Virtually all waters contain fish with salmon, sea trout (almost universally known in Ireland as white trout) and brownies found in prolific numbers across the length and breadth of the country. In addition some of the loughs also contain char populations. Frankly it's magical fish in magical surroundings but before I get too carried away with the unique charm of all things Irish – the hills, the craic, the poteen you know the sort of thing, let us focus on just why Ireland's trout are so uniquely special.

Though it has been known for some time that there appeared to be different strains of trout in Irish loughs and rivers it was the work of Dr Andrew Ferguson of Queen's University Belfast begun in the 1980s, which firmly put on the map the range of unique trout populations to be found across Ireland. After a ground breaking study on the different types of trout found in Lough Melvin, Dr Ferguson put forward the rather radical concept that the twentieth century broad brush classification *Salmo trutta* which had replaced the nineteenth century Victorian penchant for classing trout as different species like Leven, Bull or Burn trout, was too simplistic. Ferguson's studies revealed without question that the range of Irish trout which exhibit unique feeding and spawning behaviour are genetically distinct and do not interbreed. These uniquely Irish trout are listed below.

Gillaroo

The gillaroo or gilaroo (Irish for red fellow – *giolla ruadh*) first attested to in the 1700s when Twiss in his *Tour of Ireland* mentions trout which he misnames the 'gilderoy' – is a gorgeous trout of buttery gold scattered with bright crimson and gold spots dotted from the back down the flanks. Its Latin name *Salmo stomachius* means the trout has a deepened gizzard developed to digest its principal food item of freshwater snails. Though loughs like Neagh, Conn, Corrib and Mask are purported to have trout which are similarly marked, the gillaroo's acknowledged first home is Lough Melvin on the west coast of Northern Ireland. Indeed the Melvin gillaroo have a unique gene which after extensive tests across the rest of the British Isles, has not been found in any other samples. Ferguson's experiments showed conclusively that although there are other trout present, the gillaroo of Melvin did not interbreed with the other fish spawning mainly in the outflowing River Drowse. To spawn in an outflow is very unusual for wild trout as it means the little parr gillaroos must swim upstream to make the big lough (most parr swim down from their natal stream); this is a genetically inherited tendency and may explain why the gillaroo has been lost in other Irish loughs and has never made a good fish to restock elsewhere. Once in Melvin itself, the gillaroo feed for over ninety per cent of the time on the bottom taking principally snails but also shrimp and caddis and the fish like to linger in the shallows rather than cruising the deeps. Gillaroo are much prized as a sporting fish growing up to 3lb or more and are mainly caught in the latter half of the season when they feed up for spawning time. Famous Irish angler Kingsmill Moore described them as the 'panther of the water', a description they richly deserve and in the present century anglers from far and wide still come to Lough Melvin to fish for its gillaroos.

Sonaghen

In contrast to the secretive gillaroo the sonaghen, a fish unique to Lough Melvin in west Ireland, has been shown to be a prolific fish favouring an open water almost pelagic lifestyle. They spawn up in the inflowing rivers with parr descending down to the main lough which is normal behaviour for most wild brown trout except for the unusual gillaroo. Sonaghen trout, the Irish name translates as 'black fin', are descended from colonisers of the last Ice Age thirteen thousand years ago and they are smaller, more silvery, more abundant and generally freer rising than their loch compatriots, the ferox and the gillaroo. Their behaviour is also somewhat idiosyncratic for sonaghen are known for their mid water diet of plankton, midge pupae, daphnia and other small flies and nymphs. Though the fish are found in the margins they prefer the deeper holes in Melvin where they feed on the plankton collected there. They will form loose shoals in the deeper water so where you catch one there may be more. They are not a long living trout, five years at the most, and though they share the same spawning habitat as the gillaroo the degree of interbreeding of the two types of trout is very minimal.

Ferox

Although it has been established since the early nineteenth century that populations of *Salmo ferox* (also known across the UK as Lake trout and in Ireland sometimes referred to as 'Black Lough trout') exist in a number of the larger deeper inland freshwaters of the British Isles, particularly those where char are also present, it was Ferguson's research into ferox, again undertaken in Lough Melvin, which was to prove the ferox to be a truly remarkable fish. First he revealed this fish to be one of the oldest trout races to colonise Ireland, perhaps as long as fifty thousand years ago! He then showed that while the ferox shared Lough Melvin with both gillaroo and sonaghen, the ferox did not mix and would spawn in a specific area, the Glenaniff River, away from the other trout. Thus ferox were proven to be genetically and reproductively isolated and Ferguson concluded the fish to be a separate subspecies of trout. The name ferox means ferocious and as this trout lives much longer (up to fifteen years) and grows quicker to much larger weights on a diet of other smaller fish (20lb is not uncommon) it gets the deserved reputation as a fierce predator. Apart from Lough Melvin they are also found in amongst others Loughs Corrib, Mask, Conn, Tait and the Killarney Lakes. Some anglers state that the Irish ferox are rather ugly 'big headed' thin bodied fish. If that is indeed the case it is likely to be because the fish take a huge length of time to recover from spawning. This resembles Scottish ferox which when in peak condition are beautifully proportioned but if they are not fully recovered from spawning can be thin, lanky creatures.

White Trout

This is the sea trout and historically numbers of this wonderful fish have been super abundant across all of Ireland. Today the white trout is in something of a decline due to a variety of ills including pollution, loss of spawning habitat, overfishing and fish farming in coastal waters however there are still many rivers and loughs in Ireland with goodly stocks of this fish. See also River Sea Trout on page 159.

Magnificent dollaghan trout (Photo courtesy of Stevie Munn)

Dollaghan

The dollaghan is a large migratory trout averaging 4lb or so in weight but growing to perhaps 20lb or more. The fish are uniquely native to the vast Lough Neagh near Belfast. These large trout begin a spawning migration in late July when they start to leave the big lough and run up the inflowing rivers and their tributaries. The run of dollaghan will continue through September until the trout eventually begin their spawning in late October. Studies of this unique trout have come up with some interesting findings for there appears to be several distinctive types of dollaghan. First up are the buddagh also known as breddach, names which mean in Irish Gaelic the 'big fat fellow'. These are the largest trout of Lough Neagh and its rivers and with a largely piscivorous diet the fish much resemble the ferox found in Scotland's deeper lochs. For most of the time the buddagh stay out of sight in the deeps of Neagh but sometimes they are caught when they start their necessary spawning migration up the inflowing rivers like the Six Mile or the Maine. The next big migratory trout from Neagh is the 'salmon trout'. This fish is still closely related to the dollaghan but resembles a much more silver liveried species akin to a large sea trout. Like the buddagh, the salmon trout also grows into the double figure range with consummate ease. The salmon trout will mainly feed on protein-rich smaller fish but is also known to take midge pupae and molluscs. Again it is rarely caught in the big lough but can be ensnared on its migratory route upriver to spawn.

Last but of course not least is the native dollaghan itself. The Gaelic translation of the name means a 'run of fish' or perhaps 'running fish' relating to the Irish word 'dulach' which means swift running. Some true dollaghan trout are said to be slightly smaller in relative terms to the other leviathans of Neagh and have a deep golden brown glow to their flanks. Their principal diet is one of crustaceans and freshwater shrimps. Although collectively the buddagh, the salmon trout and the dollaghan are today known under the one moniker, scientific studies have shown the trout to spawn separately and maintain a genetic isolation. Whatever their creed all the Neagh trout are strong, beautifully marked fish and exhibit all the characteristics of the cautious sea trout. As a prized sporting fish they are mainly fished for at night using salmon hair wing flies and traditional wets.

151

Croneen

Coneen are another type of large migratory trout found in the River Shannon system and common in particular to Loch Derg. They much resemble sea trout being beautifully silver and studded with black spots. To catch them you will have to fish at night using sea trout flies as it is then that the fish seem to drop their guard somewhat. The origin of the name is like dollaghan, rather obscure, croneen may come from the Irish 'cron' which means brown or reddish yellow however this is not an exact description as the fish are more silver than brown.

Irish Trout in the Twenty-first Century

Given the historic abundance of amazing trout across all of Ireland coupled with the weighting of fishery management toward salmon, there has never been the interest in the sometimes unnecessary restocking of trout that has occurred in Scotland, England and to a lesser extent in Wales. In addition, the widespread introduction of American rainbow trout has not happened in Ireland in such great numbers as it has in the rest of the British Isles. While it is true to say that near the main towns and cities brown trout populations have seen some decline in number and that during the rash of fish farm enterprises in the 1980s coastal sea trout stocks fell dramatically, overall, trout remain prolific across Ireland.

However it must be said that today these fish are not without modern threats. The main pressures on Irish trout stocks come from habitat loss particularly where there is a degrading of the natural spawning areas often due to inappropriate agricultural practices.

Over enrichment of waters from phosphate ingress is also a problem especially on some of the already highly fertile loughs of Ireland. There is also an increasing threat from the introduction of alien fish species like roach and ruffe (used as live bait in coarse angling) into traditional brown trout habitat. In addition alien molluscs like the zebra mussel have lodged themselves in Lough Erne and the Shannon system and these pests are voracious plankton feeders which have severely interrupted the food chain by taking the tiny aquatic creatures usually consumed by the other native invertebrates. Finally there also still appears a need, despite the wealth of wonderful fishing available, to educate both the general and angling public about what is needed to properly conserve native fish species for generations to come. Sadly Ireland, like Scotland, appears to lag a bit behind its English and Welsh counterparts in this respect.

Chapter 15

FISHING FOR IRISH TROUT

Early Methods

The earliest methods of angling without rod and line in Ireland are virtually identical to those used in the rest of the UK. Various nets and an assortment of traps were common as were all the other less than savoury methods like spearing, otter boards, cross lines and night lines. These would be used to gather sea trout and salmon as food or as a saleable 'crop' rather than to provide sport per se. For salmon and sea trout fishing at sea or in the mouths of rivers the Irish would employ a curragh, a canoe like craft with the outer shell made of animal skin (ox was popular) and the interior shaped with wooden struts. These shallow little craft were rather similar in design to the more rounded Welsh coracle though they had more stability and could be used over far greater distances. Inevitably progress in fishing techniques has now confined the curragh like the coracle to the role of museum piece.

Rod and line angling in Ireland developed more or less in tandem with the rest of trout fishing across the UK but unlike the other countries, the Irish seemed to hide their angling lights under bushels with few anglers choosing to record their experiences in any great detail. Given the huge amount of wonderful game fishing available across the Emerald Isle this is somewhat surprising; it seems in the early days the Irish angler preferred to convey angling knowledge by the spoken rather than the written word. While by the mid nineteenth century England and Scotland were busily churning out a wide range of trout fishing related books, few such tomes appeared from across the Irish Sea. In 1832 a gloriously titled book appeared *The Angling Excursions of Gregory Greendrake Esq. in the Counties of Wicklow, Meath, Westmeath, Longford and Cavan with additions by Gregory Greendrake Esq. Dedicated to 'All honest Brothers of the Angle'*. Sadly since copies of this book are now well over a thousand pounds, the contents of it have to remain a mystery!

Happily James O'Gorman circa 1845 came up with a capable if slightly rambling snapshot of Irish angling in the book *The Practice of Angling particularly as regards Ireland*. This details a fair amount of information relating to what appear to be remarkably well established techniques of fishing wet flies on loughs and rivers. The single colour illustration in the text however is highly significant as it shows a range of neatly tied wet flies made by one Corny Gorman in 1791. This date is especially important as it indicates that quality fly tying skills were well advanced in Ireland by the late eighteenth century. The flies shown bear considerable resemblance to modern versions of wet mayfly patterns and the design of traditional Scottish loch wet flies. Given these similarities there may have been an exchange of fly tying techniques between the two countries. However I personally feel it might just be coincidence, a sort of universal Celtic fly design necessary for big wild waters containing equally wild fish. Flies were not the only angling method for sadly, O'Gorman also refers to various Irish rivers and loughs as being 'destroyed by a general system of poaching even under the eye of gentlemen living on their borders' thereby confirming the use of nets, crosslines and otters was extremely common in the eighteenth and nineteenth centuries.

Strangely dapping is not referred to once by name in O'Gorman's book which is decidedly odd. Though O'Gorman mentions having a 'throw' that is a cast with his well greased silk line, dapping per se is not mentioned. I can only think the reason for this might be to do with social stigma. Those who dapped with live insects at that time may not have been able to buy 'proper' rods, lines and artificial flies. Since O'Gorman thought himself something of a gentlemen he may have deemed dapping as not worth referring to in the course of writing his one and only fishing book. However whether the illustrious O'Gorman referred to it or not, through the course of researching this book it has become abundantly clear that all British and Irish trout fly techniques are originally derived from a form of dapping also termed 'blow line' fishing – first attested to by Walton in England during the 1600s. Some kind of dapping would therefore be the initial form of Irish rod angling practised solely for sporting purposes on both river and lough even if it is unlikely the technique actually originated there. Today dapping has managed to remain synonymous with Irish angling techniques and is still relatively popular on the big loughs like Mask, Corrib, Conn and Erne. We shall look further at the dap in the lough style section.

River Traditions

For such a small island, Ireland is positively laced with thousands of streams ranging from the Waterford waters in the south to the Donegal rivers in the north with a zillion little gems in between! Since virtually all Irish streams contain brown trout with a goodly number also featuring the sea trout (or white trout as it is known locally) the choices are endless. Often

Many Irish rivers teem with trout

the river will link into a much bigger region of loughs and tributaries. The best plan is to get yourself a good guidebook, there are several on the market, and prepare to take at least a year off work – oh if that were possible! When fishing the rivers you can take heart in knowing many of the great and good as well as many unsung heroes have gone before you yet the rivers maintain a largely unspoilt unhurried air rather like the country itself. Let's look at the skills which are involved...

Wet Fly Across the Stream

Wet fly river angling seems to have been well established right from the 1700s and over the centuries there has not been a great deal of change in this traditional technique of Irish river trout angling. O'Gorman mentions the principal tactic of the 1840s as fishing a (wet) fly across the stream to drift down on to a rising fish. He states 'If you see a fish rise, never throw directly over him; throw your line across the stream, and judge it so that the fly may come about a foot above where he rises'. Casting a fly across to the trout was in his opinion the most deadly of all methods. This approach, still much in favour with modern anglers, coincides with that era of Scottish river fishing dominated by Thomas T Stoddart who was also a strong advocate of casting across the river and letting the flies drift down to the trout. As both O'Gorman and Stoddart pre date the W C Stewart 'always upstream' revolution which began in the late 1850s, it makes sense that both agree on this aspect. O'Gorman favoured

Angling 'across and down'

two piece spliced rods of 14ft foot in length for river trouting with the wheel (reel) a foot from the end of the butt. He preferred to use a well oiled silk line rather than the twisted hair lines which were commonly used in Ireland at that time and used tapered gut leaders with only one or two flies, which he called the drop fly and the tail fly. Unfortunately it is not made clear whether the dropper was a stand out one akin to the Welsh design made with a pig's bristle or whether it was tied directly into the central line.

The use of only a few flies differs from the equivalent Scottish tactic of using a 'strap' of up to twelve flies on a cast though again social snobberies may have played a part with O'Gorman choosing to use a few patterns to be different from the masses! Favoured patterns for Irish river angling in the nineteenth century seem to centre on bushy palmered flies, various winged versions of mayfly known as green drakes and O'Gorman also lays great store on the 'Westmeath' which appears to resemble more modern eyed flies complete with what O'Gorman describes as beads for eyes and the 'Dromore' fly a pattern akin to the Dabbler. Though undoubtedly it was practised with great skill, general records are extremely scarce on old Irish river techniques. We must assume that all the aforementioned equipment or cheaper versions of it were in common use in the sporting trout angling circle during the nineteenth century and that most rod and line angling was done in the very traditional fashion of 'across and down wet fly'.

Upstream Nymph and Dry Fly

It is interesting that although both Scottish and English river trout fishers embraced upstream dry and upstream nymph/wet fly fishing with a vengeance from the late nineteenth and early twentieth centuries onward, there does not appear to have been such obsession in Ireland with using any politically correct technique on local Irish waters. In many ways this is a blessing as it has allowed generations of river trouters to cherry pick what they feel might work on their waters (see River Colbrooke) and leave aside techniques which were sometimes more to do with social pretentiousness rather than practical application. When T C Kingsmill Moore wrote his seminal tome *A Man May Fish* in 1960, a book which effectively summarised Irish trout and sea trout fishing through the first half of the twentieth century, he wrote of 'Upstream fishing must not be allowed to become a thoughtless fetish'. Instead he wrote of casting up and across in a fan shape starting with the near bank first with the object of avoiding lining any waiting trout. Practical advice indeed and his thoughts on river tactics typify the no nonsense approach favoured on many Irish rivers today.

Traditional River Flies

Kingsmill Moore was equally astute in his thoughts on fly dressing giving an expert digest on the qualities of wet flies necessary for the river. With incisive rationale he discussed the importance of light and air being trapped in a fly and further recognised the properties of the different English flies of his era. For example how border upright wing flies behaved differently in the water from say soft hackle north country patterns. Interestingly Moore describes very few established Irish river trout patterns bar the Blue Body Black Hackle which he describes as being identical to a Scottish Cairns' Fancy and an English Broughton's Point. Undoubtedly there must have been more Irish river patterns made during his lifetime but the great KM instead chooses to concentrate on established UK favourites like the Greenwell's, Orange Partridge, Hare's Ear and the Snipe and Purple. Whatever his choice of flies KM's book remains compulsory reading for all comers to river trout angling across Britain and Ireland and we will return to his writings in the sea trout and lough fishing sections.

Modern River Trout Angling

From the magical experiences I have had of Irish river trout angling I can say with all conviction that river fishing here is usually conducted in the most delightfully practical yet relaxed fashion. Local Irish anglers are extremely lucky that they have plentiful stocks of wild naturally regenerating browns to try for as sadly in many of the more industrialised rivers in England and parts of central Scotland, native fish have been largely lost and stocking is the norm. Depending on the nature of the river, especially in terms of width and speed of flow, modern anglers usually fish floating lines or sink tips on 9ft rods with 9ft tapered leaders and 3ft tippets normally 4lb but going down to as light as 1.5lb. While a number of the rivers are spate streams with delightfully peat-tinged water which assists the angler in general concealment in summer these can run very low and clear and delicate presentation is essential. Flies range from traditional wets like the Mallard and Claret, Hare's Ear Nymph or Silver Spider through to tiny dry flies like the Elk Hair Sedges, CDCs or Gnats. Fly choice depends on the water height and what's hatching. Dry fly is slightly up and across the stream rather than directly upstream as many Irish rivers are fast flowing and the line tumbles back down too quickly and spooks fish. Wet flies are still mainly fished in the time honoured across and down fashion. See River Colbrooke on page 169 for more of the fine detail.

The River Maine meets Lough Neagh

River Sea Trout – Fishing for the White Trout

Environmental problems, particularly loss of habitat and fish farm pollution, have seen a fall off in white trout numbers on some Irish streams but if you have not fished in Ireland before, this decline is not terribly noticeable and the country remains a reasonably prolific sea trout haunt. These fish average maybe 1.5lb and can grow up to 10lb in weight though these days a fish of perhaps 5lb would be a nearer the mark. Irish waters lend themselves particularly to sea trout with coastal rivers and estuaries providing ideal habitat for fish which can then run up into the comparative safety of either the vast freshwater loughs or directly into the smaller spawning tributaries. As in Scotland and Wales the main run of white trout begins in June and can go on until October though there are some exceptions to the rule with some rivers producing very large migratory trout as early as April. November is their normal spawning time.

Early writings on sea trout fishing in Ireland are not very helpful as although the white trout would have been prolifically caught in the eighteenth and nineteenth centuries not one angler seems to have differentiated between catching white or brown trout. O'Gorman does not make any reference to early techniques for migratory fish and we can only assume they were caught either on the big salmon flies or the traditional wet brown trout fly of his era. Eventually around 1960 Kingsmill Moore became the first Irish angler to record eruditely in detail methods and flies for this wonderful sporting fish. First he considered that because the white trout chases its prey at sea it would take better in the river when offered a fly on a fast retrieve. This contradicted much of the advice of his peers which centred on fishing techniques akin to catching salmon, fishing a slow fly across and down with little or no retrieve. Then he discussed what little necessity there was to exactly 'match the hatch' in order to catch these fish and instead put forward a succession of adapted English 'Bumble' patterns which were general representations eagerly snapped up by the white trout. Of these the most notable is the Claret Bumble which KM called 'an outstanding pattern for white trout' and the Fiery Brown Bumble which he thought excellent for coloured water. He also noted that migratory trout preferred a chunky thick-set body on a fly which was at the time quite different from the skinny salmon patterns being used for the 'whites'. Thus he would use a silvery winged fly on a tail fly and the bushy Bumble on the top dropper and had great success with this simple ploy: modern anglers still do!

Specialist Dollaghan Fishing

The dollaghan as we have already learned is a unique migratory trout which does not go to sea but spends its winter and spring in the largest freshwater in the British Isles, Lough Neagh, feeding in its highly rich environment. From about the beginning of July, dollaghan will enter

Dollaghan flies

the inflowing rivers and slowly head upstream to spawn in waves from late October to the following March. Given its considerable size and cautious bottom feeding behaviour the fish requires some slightly different skills in order to catch them and I was privileged to spend time in the company of top river guides Stevie Munn and Alan Kirkpatrick of the Six Mile Water and the River Maine respectively learning more about this challenging species. It is their tactics I convey to you now. As this trout grows large (4lb would be an average size) due to its piscivorous and crustacean led diet, large shrimp patterns akin to brightly coloured salmon flies seem to work best. Flies are size 4 to 8 doubles, tubes or Waddingtons and these are used with 8 to 12lb nylon with an 8 or 9 floating or sink tip line and 10ft reservoir rod; these are hefty fish! Angling is normally carried out akin to Welsh sea trout with fishing in the twilight hours into the dark of night the most popular method of ensnaring a shy cautious dollaghan. Apart from casting under banks and trees where these light sensitive fish lie this method of trout fishing is somewhat divorced from the traditional river brown trout angling as it involves working big salmon-like patterns rather than traditional trout flies. This is more like night fishing for sea trout and flies need a varied retrieve sometimes fast sometimes just a simple across and down letting the fly drift on to the nose of the fish.

An encounter with a dollaghan on the Neagh rivers is truly a trout angler's dream every bit as fabulous as catching an Irish sea trout. Because of the secretive nature of the fish I get the impression it is somewhat overlooked, I would urge you to rectify that situation.

Chapter 16

FISHING THE LOUGHS

Just as there are thousands of choice trout rivers in Ireland there are almost an equal number of loughs large and small from which to choose; the selection is beguiling and bewitching. Of course most anglers will have heard of Loughs Corrib, Mask and Conn of Eire, vast rich waters which take years to get to know properly and almost always require a knowledgeable gillie for success. These great loughs have been so celebrated in literature, Kingsmill Moore to Hugh Falkus with hundreds of others in between have propounded their glories, it is sometimes easy to forget there are some smaller equally fine if less trumpeted waters across the whole of the country from north to south. As with the Irish rivers you need lots of time, a good guidebook and the services of an expert guide will help considerably. Let's take a more in depth glance at what skills you might require…

Irish Dapping

As we have seen from English and European historical references to dapping, the first expertise may not have exactly begun on Ireland yet over the centuries this simple basic technique has remained synonymous with Irish lough fishing. Unlike its UK neighbouring countries where it has almost but not quite been forgotten, the popularity of the method has not wavered that much here. Yes wet and dry fly and nymph are now more commonly used but there are still dapping fans especially when the mayfly or daddy long legs are atop the water. Quite simply the nature of the vast Irish loughs, some of which are twenty plus miles long and studded with islands, lends itself perfectly to dapping. Most anglers fish from the boat rather than bank and with big trout lurking in rolling waves and wind slicks eager to feed on nature's bounty, dapping is often the easiest and most relaxed way of going about your angling. With such plentiful natural large insect hatches notably mayfly, fishing the dap either with the live insects or the artificial can be very successful.

It is interesting that over the years dapping with very long rod and floss (blow) line and live insects or artificials has enjoyed something of a mixed reception amongst the local or visiting angling fraternity almost since its first recognition as a technique divorced from wet fly fishing. O'Gorman, one of the few Irish anglers ever to record trout exploits writing in 1845, fails to mention dapping at all presumably because it was generally done by fishing live insects rather than artificial flies. Scottish angler Francis Francis wrote in 1867 in *A Book on Angling* that regarding dapping with live insects on Irish waters 'many clubs and good anglers do follow and profess it, and in many lakes it yields almost the only sport got from them' and went on to claim the art was so destructively good at catching trout it may not be entirely fair fishing! Oddly enough the Victorian sporting anglers visiting Ireland in the late 1800s thought it grand sport to dap, but few wrote on it. Later, Kingsmill Moore wrote eruditely on trout angling through the first half of the twentieth century yet dismisses dapping as sleep inducing calling it 'The dullest and least skilful of all methods'. A A Luce in *Fishing and Thinking* (1959) thought that dapping was 'not the most serious or most sporting form of angling; but it

Preparing to dap on Lough Erne

gets fish, and large fish'. In this he thought it a congenial relaxing way of fishing and rather nice for a family sport. Tellingly he maps a season's results for fishing with the dap and compares it to other popular Irish methods. He describes catches from Lough Conn in 1941 as thirty-seven trout caught on the dap, sixteen by the troll and 153 to the wet fly; an interesting and reasonably accurate breakdown of the success that can be achieved with this tactic.

In the twenty-first century dapping is still a feature on some of the bigger loughs especially on Mask and Erne and local anglers use an interesting set up of light coarse angling rod of about 15ft, a reel containing 8lb Maxima nylon wound directly to the reel extending along 5ft of floss tied on the core nylon with the end forming 6ft of leader to which various enormous bushy patterns are attached. Gone are the great heavy greenheart rods and huge lengths of floss, this modern set up allows the floss to billow like a skinny sail while still maintaining the integral strength of the monofilament. On its day the dap still does the business just as it did centuries ago.

Lough Style

If you take a look at how anglers fish the vast Irish loughs the techniques do not seem that much different from the rest of the UK. In many ways the methods used have developed very similarly to Scottish loch style first using wet fly teams and then the later introduction of dry fly and nymph. To avoid repetition on these aspects (most has already been recorded in the Scottish loch style section) I will concentrate on what I feel is unique to Irish lough angling. For years the Scottish loch style angler has relied heavily on using combinations of black bushy flies teamed with patterns of brilliant hue often referred to as the Gaudy fly. The Irish lough angler does this too calling it traditional wet fly fishing (see also Lough Melvin section) using teams of three or four flies fished on medium retrieve on either floating or intermediate line. However given the high lime rich fertility of many of the Irish loughs he or she also pays considerable attention to matching of the hatch especially where mayfly, daddies and/or duckfly are concerned.

Many thoughtfully designed patterns have come from Irish loughs and though they may seem on the big side compared both to smaller English lake patterns they are still brilliant imitations of the real thing. If you thought matching the hatch was purely an English phenomenon think again for Irish anglers have been doing it brilliantly since time immemorial. At mayfly time lough anglers will go afloat with boxes upon boxes of beautifully crafted mayfly imitations ranging from pale golden yellow, through various shades of olive green then another different black and white tying for the spent gnats (mayflies) which fall lifeless on the water after mating. Such fly boxes are glorious sights every bit as exciting as the millions of graceful natural insects you can see in various stages

Lough style on Melvin

of emerging, drying their wings, mating or dying. More on mayfly fishing appears in the review of Lough Erne.

Today the modern lough angler will use an eclectic combination of flies largely according to the season. Anything from a Bibio, a Dabbler or an Octopus will feature happily beside an Anderson's Spent Gnat, a big Murrough or a Yellow Wulff. Irish anglers tend to go for what suits the conditions and what's hatching rather than because the fly might be the latest fashion accessory, a welcome approach in the sometimes daft world of the stockie basher with huge lures and lead core lines.

The White Trout of the Lough

Fishing for sea trout is mainly centred on the more acidic waters scattered along the west of Northern and Southern Ireland. Lough angling is largely though not exclusively done by the boat and a good dark overcast blowy day is best as the Irish white trout are easily spooked creatures just as canny here as they are elsewhere. Teams of flies are used much akin to Scottish loch sea trout fishing and these are worked on floating or intermediate lines with a medium to fast paced retrieve. The white trout like something to chase and an old gillie's trick (also common in Scotland) is to use a flashy lure like fly on the end of the cast and a bushy black top dropper. This to a waiting trout looks like a small fish chasing a fast moving prey and the white trout might just nip in to intercept it – on the other hand it might not but it's worth a try! Dibbling the top dropper before lifting off is common and dapping for the big sea trout also has its charms. Night fishing is also done for white trout but since Irish loughs are dangerous rocky places when you are unfamiliar with the layout if you try this it is preferable to have a guide with you. Flies are very traditional with Bibio, Pennell, various Bumbles especially the Claret Bumble, Silver Invicta, Teal Blue and Silver and the Zulu all employed in sizes 8 to 12. White trout will also seize a big mayfly imitation either dapped or fished dry so there is plenty of scope for experimentation.

Chapter 17

CORNERSTONES OF IRISH TROUT FISHING

To give you a taste of Irish trout fishing is almost an impossible job. Quite simply the trout of Ireland are wonderfully abundant, diverse creatures and the thousands of waters they inhabit cannot be recorded. Since most anglers even if they have never visited Ireland will have heard of the loughs of Corrib, Mask, Conn, Sheelin, Derg and Ennell with their fabulous mayfly and duckfly fishing and the great rivers like the Moy, Bann, Foyle, Finn or Delphi mainly in connection with their salmon runs, I thought it would be better to feature some of the lesser sung gems which dot this lovely country from end to end. Where to begin is difficult but as I have researched these waters with generous help from locals on the ground I feel it is best to write about what I have personally experienced so there now follow some snapshots of the fabulous trout angling this country offers.

Lough Melvin

Ever since I first read of Lough Melvin with its wonderfully spotted gillaroo and those grey flanked black finned sonaghan not to mention the ferox that lurk in its depths, it has been my continued ambition to fish there. In 2005 that dream was finally realised when the chance came to visit this enigmatic water as part of the research for this book. To say the prospect of following in the footsteps of the great Kingsmill Moore and many other supreme anglers was thrilling was putting it mildly and it was in a state rather akin to an overexcited schoolgirl that I at last arrived on the shores of this wonderful lough.

Melvin lay calm and blue nestled in trees below the long buttress of low hills which guard the south shore at Rossinver as I met up with Irish internationalist Ruth Mettler and gillie Joe Gallagher both locals of Melvin who so kindly took time to show me the ropes of the lough. Perhaps the first thing that sets this lough apart from others is its darker slightly peat-stained water, so different from the other lime rich waters of the south of Ireland. In this Melvin looked remarkably similar to some of Scotland's more acidic lochs except that all the shores were deeply tree lined, whereas in Scotland trees on many loch shores have long since disappeared, overgrazed by deer and removed for fuel and timber. The feeding for the trout of Melvin is less prolific than other Irish waters with a much smaller variety of insects hatching. Small midge, sedge and stonefly with a tiny sprinkle of mayfly were on the go that hot bright May day but my companions told me that the feeding generally does not get much more profuse than what was on the go that day.

A gillaroo was our first quest and we spent a couple of hours hugging the shoreline fishing with flies like the size 10 Green Peter, Bibio and bright orange Bumble. The gillaroo hugs the bottom consuming snail, caddis and shrimp and our tactics were with intermediate lines and teams of three flies. These were fished on medium to fast retrieve with the usual dibbling of the top dropper and it was a pleasure to watch Ruth work those flies with consummate ease close to the bank. Unfortunately any trout that did take refused to stay on the end of the line and since I was fishing with the best we put failure down to the increasing sunshine and cloudless

Ruth and Joe at home on Melvin

skies. Trout are shy in these conditions at the best of times but gillaroo are notorious for keeping well out of sight of bright light. Instead we turned our attention to the sonaghan which lurk out mid water especially near to the little skerries and deep drop offs. Flies were switched to the Octopus and the Dabbler, again yellow and gold seemed the most favoured colours rather than black flies. A few of these daphnia feeders did show but with the lough remaining a mill pond they too remained shy and retiring with takes quickly shaken free of the hook.

So what do sensible anglers who have come to fish from so far away do (apart from retire to the nearest hostelry which wasn't an easy option) when the conditions are so set against them? Talk of course so the discussions were long and wide ranging on everything concerning Melvin and its fish. For a start it seems that the Irish stalwart's technique of dapping has never been particularly popular on this lough owing to its lack of sufficient numbers of hatching large insects like the mayfly. Apparently most of the trout seek their food supply underwater and do not rise much to the dap. It appeared the best conditions for gillaroo were really rough weather with drifts set close in and parallel to the shore with the gillie holding the drift by sticking the engine in reverse. I learned that most anglers fish the intermediate line rather than the floater on Melvin to get their flies where the fish are feeding more quickly.

Leaving the charming company of Ruth and Joe that day I reflected again how Irish anglers were so practical in changing and/or adapting their tactics to suit the water they are fishing and the species they are after. There I was expecting dapping and traditional floating line only to find the techniques for Melvin were subtly different. I must return when the weather is more like fishing and less like getting a sun tan....

167

Into a fish on the Colbrooke

River Colbrooke

Brown trout river fishing in Ireland is hugely underrated. In the rush to meet the lough mayfly, grab a salmon or nab a perch (this country is as famed for its coarse angling as its game fishing) trout in rivers are generally neglected. This is a great pity as the sport they can offer is tremendous and every bit as good as lough fishing and in a much smaller less daunting setting. Think babbling brooks rather than raging seas and you just about have it. In addition the river trout are far less affected by the conditions of brilliant sunshine which sometimes send the lough trout running for cover. With many rivers tree lined and lush with plenty of glides, streamy runs and deep shady pools, this is the ideal habitat for trout.

River trout fishing is in short great at any time but is a more than creditable alternative when the loughs are proving dour. It was during such a period that I took time out to fish the excellent River Colbrooke at Maguiresbridge. Here I was lucky enough to spend a few hours in the esteemed company of local river guide Patrick Trotter who lives in the village. First I learned that my lough tackle, if not completely wrong for the river, needed a fair bit of tweaking to be useful. Off came the ordinary 9ft 4lb nylon leader which I was told was not turning over quick enough to produce the neatest presentation to the wary trout – think about it; in a lough you can launch out a three fly team with wind behind and everything gets straightened out when you start your retrieve, in a river you need the fly leader and line all to be in immediate contact before the current causes the leader to be pulled in all directions. On went a 9ft tapered leader with 3ft tippet going down to as light as 1.5lb. This immediately made a difference with the quicker line turnover putting the fly almost directly where the fish where rising rather than sometimes collapsing short.

Next my smallest flies (size 16 Wickhams) were removed and replaced with flies like the Griffiths Gnat, a whiskery version of an Adams without a wing. This fly was highly visible on

Whiskery delicacies for the Colbrooke

the water – well it was to Patrick, who could spot it instantly amongst a mass of small midges buzzing about close to the water surface. This was cast across and slightly ahead of the fish so that the trout saw the fly rather than line. Before Patrick arrived I had been trying to fish my dry fly upstream in time honoured fashion but was told in highly practical fashion that this could line the trout and therefore an across stream cast starting close then working out across the pool was better as indeed it was! This again highlighted the practical approach that anglers have to their fishing in Ireland; you must forget fashion here or fail.

The main feeding for the trout in the Colbrooke is a mix of midge, olives, mayfly, sedges, spinners, yellow may dun and trout also take caddis and small crayfish. The pH of the water is neutral to slightly alkaline and though the average size of fish may be smaller when compared to the lough leviathans, about ¾lb to 1lb is the norm; they still grow well and fight like tigers twice their size. Lake trout also venture into the Colbrooke from Lough Erne running upstream to spawn and these can range anything from 6lb to 12lb in weight. The river also has one overriding benefit – there are few if any salmon present. This means poaching is rarely seen and the fish are largely left in peace. The trout population flourishes with a wide range of sizes from a few ounces to several pounds in weight, always an extremely healthy sign. At £5.00 per day ticket this is the place to spend heavenly hours undisturbed flicking a fly between the trees and admiring the golden beauties which you catch. Even better, get that esteemed fishing guide Patrick Trotter to show you the ropes, watch and learn – a real touch of Irish magic!

Lower Lough Erne

It is a difficult task to describe fully this vast island-studded lough; think a chequered history stretching back to Viking times, think wild waters and sheltered tree-lined bays, think food-rich slicks and foaming wind lanes, think thick carpets of Green Drakes, think big secretive trout kissing the surface flies, think over thirty-seven thousand acres of fishing heaven and you just about have it. Not that this is easy angling for Lower Lough Erne can be notoriously difficult with hefty trout that switch themselves on and off the feed in a blink of an eye. Altogether Erne is perhaps a lough for the big boys and girls, often you will need to really work for your fish but when you do catch them look out for an average sized trout of maybe 2lb with specimens of 5lb plus relatively commonplace. The challenging nature of this water goes before it and there are some telling statistics attached to Erne worth repeating here. Seems that while around seventy per cent of locals game fish here the remaining thirty per cent angle for coarse species like pike and perch. However these figures are completely reversed when you look at visiting fishers with seventy per cent of the visitors going after coarse fish and only around thirty per cent chasing the big trout. This may be because of the huge amount of publicity given to coarse fishing in Ireland or simply because of the daunting size of Erne where a good boat and a good gillie are essential to stand any chance of being successful.

Bearing all this in mind I was fortunate to meet up with expert local fishing guide Colin Chartres who, having been born and raised in this picturesque area, knows the lough in all its moods. Colin took time to explain the nature of this lime rich water with its ninety-seven islands, rocky outcrops and drop offs which can go down to 200ft or more. In order to find any feeding trout we were going to have to explore the edges of the islands especially the wind slicks of calmer water formed at the back of these green tree covered havens. Trout will often grab your fly only a couple of feet from the shore and it quickly became obvious that the electric gillie (an electric motor placed astern beside the main petrol motor) is very much needed here to hold the boat close in to the shore. Colin also went through the flies necessary for my May visit intentionally timed to coincide with the first fall of mayfly. For day fishing the local anglers use flies like the Mosely May ingeniously tied flat to look like a spent natural, and also the Erne Mayfly and the O'Conner's Yellow or Green Mayfly made on Limerick hooks which have a slightly offset barb and hook. These shaped hooks are said to be better at holding on to the Erne leviathans. Looking at the serried ranks of these lovely flies it quickly became obvious the Irish take their mayfly time very seriously and if that wasn't enough, had we been fishing at night we would have been using different black and white versions of spent flies notably Anderson's Spent Gnat which is the most popular night fly on Erne.

While early in the season the main tactics for this lough which opens on 1 March, centre on working teams of traditional wets like Fiery Browns, Hare's Ears or Dabblers on intermediate or ghost tip lines on drifts close to the shore, with the mayfly up in mid May we used dry flies on floating lines along with the occasional dapped fly. It was interesting that Colin and only one or two other local enthusiasts still use the dap on Erne, it seems very much that this old tradition has largely been replaced by the dry fly or teams of wets. I loved the tales of the old customs of fishing the live mayfly, two on a hook with a brilliant yellow gorse petal sandwiched between to add colour. Also the legend of only starting to fish the mayfly once the white thorn trees are fully in bloom, great stuff! From about 12th May many local anglers fish Erne for the mayfly 'duffers fortnight' which continues for three or four weeks after which there is a lull before a secondary hatch of mayfly around 20th July which lasts for about two weeks. In between hatches of the bigger flies, sedge and olive imitations

Lower Lough Erne

Colin changes tactics on Erne

Magnifcent Erne trout

are fished and then in late August through to the close on 30th September anglers revert to deeper water tactics mainly with traditional wets like the Green Peter or the Octopus.

Listening to all this information from Colin it quickly became apparent how much store the Irish lough angler places upon following the rhythm of seasons switching artificials according to predominant hatch, so different from the sometimes unsubtle tactics used on stocked reservoirs. It's not all roses though because an unwelcome invasion of the zebra mussel emanating from the Shannon system has meant the trout are now feeding more and more on bottom fodder. Seems the alien mussel pests have caused a clarification of the water which has in turn increased weed growth at deeper levels and shrimp and hog louse have now reached record numbers in Erne. With such a lush carpet of trout food on the lough floor local anglers say the fish have become even more difficult to catch as they are steadfastly refusing to rise in the numbers they once did. Despite this it's still a fabulous place to fish and Colin led the way with a fine trout from the Rosscor area caught on the Mosely May. As for me – well I had my chances but failed to get anything to stay on even during a spectacular mayfly hatch which saw several enormous trout cruising upwind into a fine slick of water between two islands gobbling up the struggling insects with electrifying splashes and slurps which made this angler's hair stand on end. It's easy to see why so many anglers become bewitched by the challenge of the Erne and I urge you to join their ranks sooner rather than later…

SECTION 5

THE FLIES

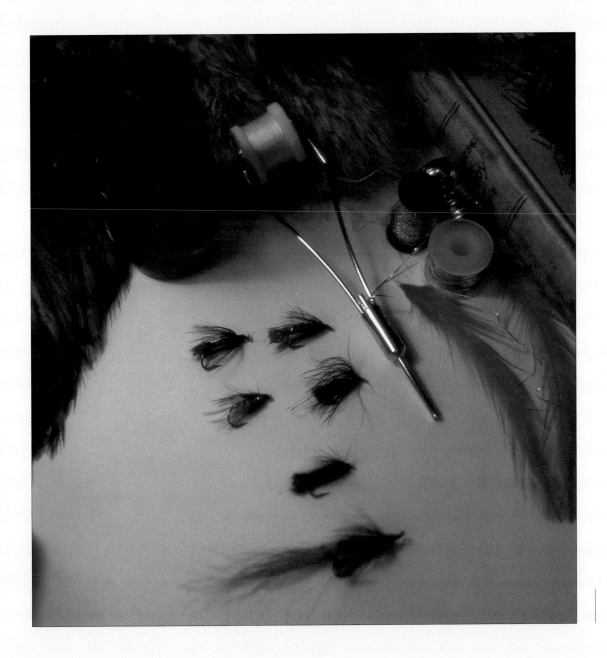

This section contains standard dressings for selected flies mentioned in the text. The originator of the fly is given where known and/or a particular water is indicated where the pattern would be most often used. Some patterns are tied in a signature style for example 'Clyde Style' or 'Edmonds and Lee' and this again is indicated where known. This information is meant to give a general indication however and should not be taken as written in tablets of stone. Many of today's successful flies from across the UK and Ireland are derivatives and variants of ancient patterns or were originally designed for a specific lake or river but have gone on to be universally used.

Scottish Specials

Badger and Red (River Tweed favourite) size 14 for dry fly.
Body – red silk
Hackle – badger cock hackle
Tail – a few badger hackle fibres

Badger Palmer (old traditional loch fly) size 8 to 12 for dapping, 10 to 16 for wet fly.
Body – mixed hare's ear and mole's fur
Rib – gold tinsel or brown silk
Hackle – thickly palmered badger cock hackle, add extra hackle at head for dapping fly.

Black Nymph (R C Bridgett) size 12 to 16 wet loch fly.
Body – black ostrich herl
Rib – fine silver
Hackle – soft speckled guinea hen
Tail – a few fibres guinea hen

Black Palmer (old traditional loch fly) size 8 to 12 for dapping, 10 to 16 for wet loch fly.
Body – black ostrich herl
Rib – gold wire
Hackle – palmered black cock hackle, extra head hackle for dapping fly

Black Spider (W C Stewart) size 12 to 16 wet river and loch fly.
Body – waxed brown tying silk
Hackle – cock starling neck feather softly palmered only at head

Cinnamon Fly (W Murdoch) size 10 to 16 wet fly mainly lochs.
Body – dark cinnamon seal's fur or substitute
Rib – silver thread
Hackle – black and red cock hackle at head only
Wings – cinnamon brown hen or partridge
Tail – a few fibres of red cock hackle
Tag – oval silver tinsel

Dun Spider (W C Stewart) size 12 to 16 wet river or loch fly.
Body – pale brown tying silk waxed
Hackle – small inside wing feather of starling lightly palmered at head.

Green Mantle (W Murdoch) size 10 to 14 wet loch fly.
Body – bright green seal's fur or substitute
Hackle – green cock hackle palmered all the way down the body
Wings – dark mallard in double strips or rolled wing
Tail – GP topping
Tag – oval tinsel

Green Nymph (R C Bridgett) size 12 to 16 wet loch fly.
Body – swan herl dyed apple green or substitute
Rib – fine gold
Hackle – olive hen
Tail – a few fibres olive hen

177

Greenwell's Glory (Tweed origin but now universally used across the UK)
size 12 to 16 wet river and loch fly.
Body – waxed yellow silk
Rib – gold thread
Hackle – Coch Y Bondhu hen hackle lightly tied at the head
Wing – starling

Hen Blackie (Clyde style) size 12 to 16 wet river fly.
Body – yellow silk lightly waxed
Hackle – black hen
Wing – hen blackbird dressed flat along the hook shank

Ke He (20th century Orkney loch fly) size 10 to 14 wet river fly.
Body – plump peacock herl
Rib – fine gold wire lightly tied
Hackle – dark ginger hen tied long
Tail – red wool under slim GP tippets

Leven Spider (modern Loch Leven origin)
size 10 to 14 wet loch fly.
Body – flat gold
Rib – fine oval gold or fine wire
Hackle – sparse short black hen
Tail – lime green fluorescent floss

Loch Ordie (old traditional loch fly) size 8 to 12 dapping, wet fly sizes 10 to 16.
Body – brown tying silk
Hackles – thickly palmered red brown and ginger hackles
Head hackle – white hackle over wound to finish

Olive Nymph (R C Bridgett) size 12 to 16 wet loch fly.
Body – swan herl dyed medium olive or substitute
Rib – fine gold wire
Hackle – blue hen
Tail – a few fibres of blue hen

Peter Ross (20th century traditional loch fly) size 10 to 14 wet fly.
Body – upper red seal's fur, lower flat or oval silver tinsel
Rib – fine silver wire
Head hackle – black hen
Wing – barred teal
Tail – a few GP tippets

Red Palmer and Soldier Palmer (old traditional loch fly) size 8 to 12 for dapping flies, 10 to 16 for wet fly.
Body – red wool or red seal's fur
Rib – gold tinsel
Palmered hackle – red brown cock hackle, extra head hackle for dapping fly
Tail – red wool (Soldier Palmer only)

Sand Fly (Clyde style) size 14 wet river fly.
Body – black silk lightly dubbed with mole fur
Hackle – black hen not more than two turns

Sand Fly (Clyde style dry) size 14 or 16 dry river fly.
Body – lightly dubbed mole fur on black tying silk
Hackle – brown partridge over a longish black cock hackle

Shilfie Tip (Clyde style) size 14 or 16 wet river fly.
Body – black silk
Hackle – small black hen
Wing – secondary feather from the chaffinch with light coloured edging, set upright

White Tip (W Murdoch) size 10 to 16 wet loch fly.
Body – two turns of yellow the rest black seal's fur well picked out
Rib – broad oval silver tinsel
Hackle – black cock hackle
Wings – white tip mallard with a good green sheen
Tail – GP topping

English Elite

Ace of Spades (Dave Collyer) size 6 to 10 long shank modern wet lake fly.
Body – black chenille
Rib – oval silver tinsel
Wing – black hen hackle tied streamer fashion
Over wing – dark mallard
Throat hackle – guinea fowl

Alexandra (possibly Turle or Brunton) size 10 to 14 wet lake fly from the 1860s.
Body – flat silver tinsel
Rib – fine silver wire
Cheeks – strips of red feather on either side of the therl
Head hackle – black hen
Tail – red feather tippet
Wing – a few strands of green peacock herl

Appetiser (Bob Church) size 8 long shank modern wet lake fly.
Body – white chenille
Rib – fine silver tinsel
Wing – white turkey marabou
Over wing – grey squirrel
Tail – mix of green, orange and yellow cock hackle fibres

Bare Hook Nymph (Oliver Kite) size 14 to 16 minimalist river nymph fly.
Body – hook shaft
Abdomen and thorax – shaped copper wire

Black Gnat (E M Tod dressing of ancient river fly also used on stillwaters) size 12 to 18 wet fly.
Body – black silk
Head hackle – sparse black hen
Wing – pale starling wing

Black Emerger Buzzer (modern reservoir midge imitation) size 12 to 18 wet.
Abdomen – black fur with a mix of red yellow and claret fur delicately included
Rib – strand of Lureflash Crystal Hair
Wing buds – jungle cock eyes
Thorax – bronze peacock herl

Black and Peacock Spider (old river and lake fly) size 10 to 16 wet fly.
Body – bronze peacock herl wound rather fat to make plump body
Head hackle – sooty black herl hackle feather

| *Damsel fly*

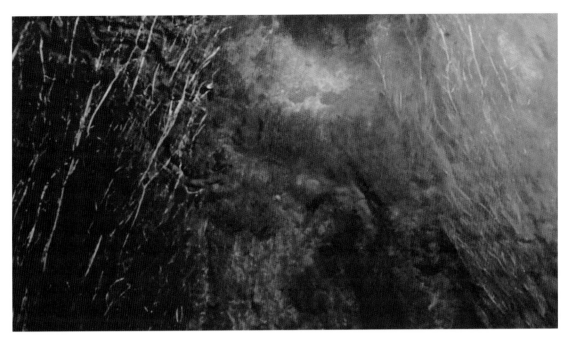

Typical chalk stream habitat

Blagdon Buzzer (modern stillwater fly dressed by Dr H A Bell) size 10 to12 wet fly.
Body – black wool slightly tapered
Rib – flat gold
Breathing filaments – bunch of white floss silk tied on the top of the hook directly behind the eye

Butcher (Moon circa 1838) size 10 to 14 wet fly usually stillwater but can be used on river in spate.
Body – flat silver tinsel
Head hackle – sparse black hen
Wings – blue sheen mallard or crow quill feather two paired sections
Tail – red feather fibres

Daddy Long Legs
Body – brown floss
Legs – strong knotted black or grey nylon mono
Hackle – ginger cock
Wing – ginger cock hackle tips tied spent

Damsel Nymph (modern version) size 8 to10 wet lake lure fly.
Body – dubbed olive marabou
Rib – fine gold or copper wire
Wing case – olive feather fibres
Tail – tuft of olive marabou
Thorax – olive marabou tied thick
Legs – more olive marabou fibres
Eyes – brown or black beads

Dark Needle (from Edmonds and Lee) size 12 to 16 river wet fly.
Body – orange brown silk
Head – magpie herl
Head hackle – brown feather from hind part of starling wing where it joins the body

Dark Watchet (from Edmonds and Lee) size 12 to 16 wet river fly.
Body – orange and purple silk twisted together and dubbed lightly with mole fur. The orange and purple silk should show in alternate strips
Head – orange silk
Head hackle – dark smoky blue feather from jackdaw throat

181

February Red (ancient fly first noted in the Treatise *as the Dun Fly)* size 14 to 16 wet river fly.

Body – medium orange tying silk and red/brown fur or light wool
Hackle – dark grizzle dun cock
Wing – centre feather of partridge tail or speckled hen wing

Floss Bloodworm size 14 to 16 wet fly midge larvae imitation for lake fishing.

Body – 2 to cm long fluorescent red floss knotted at either end and wound along hook shank
Rib – red thread
Head – 2 turns bronze peacock herl

Footballer (Geoffrey Bucknall) size 8 to 16 standard or caddis hook, 1960s wet lake fly.

Body – stripped black and white hackle stalks wound side by side, wound from tips to make thick thorax at the head of the fly
Thorax – grey seal's fur or substitute
Head – bronze peacock herl
Tail – white fluorescent floss
Breathing tubes – tuft of white fluoro floss tied forward over the hook eye

Ginger Quill (old river fly favoured by Skues and many others) size 14 to 16 wet river fly.

Body – peacock quill
Hackle – ginger cock hackle
Tail – ginger cock hackle fibres

Great Red Sedge (Dave Collyer) size 6 to 10 lake dry fly.

Body – grey mole's fur palmered with a dark red cock hackle
Rib – gold wire
Head hackle – dark red cock hackle
Wing – brown speckled hen tied sloping not longer than the hook bend
Tail – a few red cock hackle fibres

Green Mayfly (Halford) size 12 to 16 river dry fly.

Body – raffia with six turns at the tail
Rib – five turns ribbing the body with medium cinnamon horsehair (thread can be substituted)
Head hackle – golden pheasant hen
Shoulder hackle – two pale cream cock hackles
Wings – mallard of pale grey green colour.
Whisk – dark brown gallina

Hare's Ear Nymph (also known as Gold Ribbed Hare's Ear) size 12 to 16 river and lake fly.

Body – dark fur from base of hare's ear spun on dull yellow tying silk
Rib – flat gold tinsel
Legs – make the legs from the dubbed hare's ear well picked out
Tail – (optional) three long strands of hare fibres

Hare's Ear two wire Buzzer (modern version of midge pupae) size 14 to 18.

Abdomen – one strand red copper wire twisted together with a strand of dark brown copper wire. The two wires are wound round the body to look like segments
Under Thorax – small ball formed with red copper wire
Over Thorax – hare's ear fur dubbed to the wire

Hopper – Black (modern lake fly tied first by Bristol anglers) size 10 to 12 lake fly can be tied in different colours but principal is the same.

Body – black seal's fur or substitute
Rib – fine oval silver or fine mono
Hackle – black hen straggly and not too bunched
Legs – siz knotted pheasant tail fibres dyed black, 3 each side of fly

Jersey Herd (Tom Ivens) size 8 to 10 longshank stillwater lure.

Body – underlay of wool and overlaid with copper coloured tinsel or lurex

Head, back and tail – bronze peacock herl run along the upper back from head to tail

Throat hackle – hot orange cock hackle

Killer Bug (Frank Sawyer) size 8 to 14 river nymph fly often used for grayling.

Body – lead or copper wire overlaid with three layers beige wool

Rib (optional) – fine copper wire

Kite's Imperial (Oliver Kite) size 14 to 16 river dry fly also effective on lakes.

Body – natural heron herl

Rib – gold wire

Thorax – heron herl doubled and redoubled

Hackle – honey dun or light ginger cock

Tail – grey or brown hackle fibres

Light Needle (from Edmonds and Lee) size 12 to 16 wet river fly.

Body – orange silk

Head hackle – sparse feather from young starling's thigh or flank

Head – orange silk

Little Marryat (Marryat) size 12 to 18 pale watery dun imitation river fly.

Body – Opossum flank fur or substitute

Head hackle – pale buff cock

Wings – Pale starling

Tail – a few fibres of buff cock hackle

March Brown (old river fly related to Dun Fly of the Treatise) size 12 to 14 wet river fly.

Body – brown seal's fur or hares ear fur

Rib – gold wire

Hackle – brown partridge

Wings – brown hen pheasant or partridge

Tail – partridge tail fibres

Medicine (modern Falkus favourite) size 6 to 10 sea trout fly.
Body – silver paint on the hook or very fine silver tinsel
Wing – brown flank feathers of mallard drake folded to form a sparse fibre bundle
Head hackle – blue cock hackle tied sparse
Head – varnished red tying silk

Partridge and Orange (north country origin) size 12 to 16 wet river fly.
Body – orange tying silk
Rib – optional gold tinsel or gold wire
Hackle – soft dark speckled partridge

Red Spinner (Marryat) size 12 to 18 dry fly.
Body – peacock quill
Rib – fine gold wire
Hackle – black butted red cock hackle
Wings – honey dun
Tail – a few fibres of pale cream cock hackle

Sawyer's Pheasant Tail Nymph (Frank Sawyer) size 12 to 16 wet river and lake fly.
Under body – copper wire along the hook with extra hump for the thorax
Over body – pheasant tail fibres wound with the wire and tied thick at thorax
Wing case – pheasant tail fibres doubled over
Tail – three cock hackle fibres

Shipman's Buzzer (Dave Shipman) size 10 to 14 modern lake fly midge imitation.
Body – fiery brown seal's fur
Rib – medium gold flat tinsel
Breathing filaments – white wool tied in at head and tail

Skues' Pheasant Tail Nymph (G M Skues) size 12 to 16 wet river fly.
Body – three or four strands of herl from ruddy part of centre feather of cock pheasant tail
Rib – fine bright gold wire
Wings – golden dun cock's hackle of good colour
Whisks – honey dun cock shoulder hackle three strands

Snipe and Purple (from Edmonds asnd Lee) size 12 to 16 wet river fly.
Body – purple silk
Head hackle – dark feather from snipe wing
Head – purple silk tied slightly thicker to form head

Stick Fly (Collyer) size 8 to10 modern stillwater caddis fly imitation.
Body – dark pheasant tail fibres mixed with olive swan herls
Rib – copper, silver or gold tinsel wound opposite to the body herls ribbed with peacock herl
Hackle – sparse pale ginger cock
Thorax – yellow or off white floss
Head – varnished black or dark olive tying silk

Tup's Indispensable (Austin version 1900, later refined by Skues) size 12 to 16 river dry fly.
Body – a mix of white fur from ram's testicle, lemon fur from spaniel, cream seal's fur and yellow mohair
Hackle – yellow spangled light blue cock hackle
Tail – a few fibres of same hackle

Tup's (Taff Price) size 12 to 16 modern version of the famous river fly.
Body – rear half yellow floss
Thorax – mix of yellow, red and honey coloured seal's fur
Hackle – honey dun cock hackle

Waterhen Bloa (old north country river fly) size 12 to 16 wet river fly.
Body – primrose yellow tying silk dubbed sparse with a mix of blue rabbit underfur and mole
Hackle – waterhen wing feather sparse

Winter Brown (from Edmonds and Lee) size 12 to 16 wet river fly.
Body – orange silk dubbed with ruddy brown wool but keeping an orange flash at the tail
Head – bronze peacock herl
Head hackle – grey feather barred from the under coverts of a woodcock's wing with lighter side at the head of the fly.

185

Welsh Wonders

Allrounder size 6 to 8 sewin river fly principally for night fishing.
Body – black seal's fur or substitute
Rib – silver thread
Hackle – black cock hackle
Wing – black squirrel with red squirrel overlaid
Tail – GP topping
Cheeks – jungle cock
Topping – peacock sword feathers

Black and Silver size 8 to 12 single, double or tube river wet fly.
Body – flat silver tinsel
Hackle – black hen tied long
Rib – silver wire

Blue Black and Silver size 4 to 10 river sewin fly.
Body – silver tinsel
Rib – silver wire
Hackle – blue or black
Wing – black, blue and natural squirrel

Blue Hen (Dai Lewis) size 12 to 14 river wet fly.
Body – black quill tied fine
Hackle – underwing of moorhen (summer plumage)
Thorax – black herl

Blue Black and Silver size 4 to 10 sewin river fly tied on single, tandem, tube or with flying treble.
Body – Silver tinsel
Rib – silver wire
Hackle – blue or black
Wing – black squirrel

Brown and Yellow Mole size 4 to 6 Towy river sewin fly.
Body – front two-thirds mole fur, rear yellow wool
Rib – gold wire
Hackle – ginger
Wing – brown hen or turkey
Tag – yellow wool

Cob, Brecon size 12 to14 river wet fly. Note the March Brown is known as the Cob at Brecon.
Body – dark red seal's fur or silk
Rib – gold wire
Hackle – dark partridge hackle
Wing – hen pheasant wing

Coch-a-bon-ddu (also spelt Coch Y Bondhu and similar) size 8 to 12 river and lake wet fly.
Body – peacock herl
Rib – fine gold wire
Hackle – furnace or Coch

Dai's Alder size 12 River Teifi dry fly.
Body – peacock herl
Hackle – two black cock hackles
Front hackle – grouse feather

Diawl Bach size 10 to 14 lake and reservoir wet fly.
Body – peacock herl tied full or skinny (anorexic)
Rib – Red, gold or silver
Throat hackle – red game cock hackles
Tail – red game cock hackle fibres

Haul a Gwynt size 12 to14 lake wet fly.
Body – black ostrich herl
Hackle – small cock pheasant neck feathers
Wing – black crow

Orl size 12 to 14 River Teifi wet fly also used on Welsh lakes.
Body – peacock herl
Rib – red tying silk
Hackle – blue dun

Paragon (Dai Lewis) size 12 to 14 river dry fly.
Body – rabbit face
Hackle – two dark brown Rhode Island hen hackles tied full
Tail – dark red cock fibres

Secret Weapon size 6 to 8 sewin fly tied with small flying treble.
Body – silver tinsel
Rib – silver tinsel
Hackle – blue
Wing – dark or mixed squirrel

Sunk Lure size 6 to 8 tandem hooks.
Adaptation of single hook sewin/sea trout fly like the Teal Blue and Silver or the Alexandra dressing made on tandem hooks

Teal Blue and Silver size 6 to 12 single, tandem, tube or flying treble style river sewin wet fly.
Body – flat silver tinsel
Rib – silver wire
Hackle – blue
Wing – speckled teal breast or flank feathers
Tail – GP tippets

Teifi Terror size 6 to 10 tandem hook daylight sewin fly fished on the falling flood.
Body – black floss
Rib – gold wire
Hackle – furnace
Tail – furnace cock fibres

Usk Purple size 12 to 14 River Usk wet fly.
Body – purple floss
Hackle – dark blue dun
Wing – snipe wing

Welshman's Button (Tom Tom) size 12 river and lake dry fly.
Body – peacock herl sometimes with a yellow floss twist in centre
Hackle – red and black game mixed tied full

Irish Favourites

Amber Dabbler size 10 to 12 lough wet fly.
Body – golden olive and orange seal's fur
    mixed
Rib – broad oval gold
Hackle – red game
Wing – bronze mallard
Tail – cock pheasant fibres

Anderson's Spent Gnat size 8 –to 10
longshank dry lough fly (for mayfly).
Body – white floss overlaid with clear plastic
    sheath
Rib – peacock quill or black thread
Hackle – barred red cock trimmed
    underneath to make fly fall spent
Body hackle – short iron blue cock hackle
Underwing – 2 barred rock cock hackle tips
    tied spent
Overwing – 2 iron blue cock hackle tips tied
    spent
Tail – three fibres cock pheasant dyed black

Bibio size 8 to 14 wet lough fly for both sea
and brown trout.
Body – black seal's fur with a hot orange or
    red centre spot
Rib – fine oval silver
Hackle – two palmered black cock hackles

Bibio

Claret Bumble size 8 to12 wet lough fly for
sea and brown trout.
Body – claret seal's fur or substitute
Rib – oval gold tinsel
Hackle – palmered claret and black cock hackle
Front hackle – blue jay
Tail – GP tippets

Claret Dabbler size 8 to 10 wet lough fly.
Body – claret seal's fur
Rib – fine oval gold tinsel
Hackle – ginger cock palmered with light
    claret cock hackle at shoulder
Wing – slips of bronze mallard tied around
    the body reaching to the tail
Tail – cock pheasant tail fibres

Dromore (O'Gorman description 1845)
size 8 to 10 river and lough wet fly.
Body – claret or brown seal's fur
Rib – silver tinsel
Shoulder hackle – red or grey
Wing – peacock breast feather with mallard
Tail – pheasant tail fibres apparently dyed
olive green

*Fiery Brown Bumble (Kingsmill Moore
favourite)* size 8 to 12 river and lough
sea/brown wet fly.
Body – fiery brown seal's fur
Body hackle – palmered fiery brown and red
    cock hackle
Tail – Indian crow
Tag – golden brown floss
Shoulder Hackle – dark grouse

*Golden Olive Bumble (Kingsmill Moore
favourite)* size 10 to 12 lough wet fly.
Body – red seal's fur butt; golden olive seals
    fur main body
Rib – broad golden oval tinsel
Body hackle – one golden olive hackle and
    one bright yellow palmered together
Front hackle – blue jay
Tail – GP crest

Green Peter size 8 to 10 wet lough fly.
Body – green or olive seal's fur
Rib – gold tinsel or wire
Hackle – light olive or ginger cock hackle
Wing – pheasant tail or pheasant wing

Griffith's Gnat size 14 to 18 river dry fly.
Body – sparse peacock herl
Hackle – palmered sparse natural grizzle
Thread – black or grey

Kingsmill (Kingsmill Moore) size 8 to 12 wet lough fly.
Body – black ostrich herl
Rib – oval silver
Hackle – black cock hackle
Wing – rook secondary rolled
Tail – GP topping
Tag – gentian blue floss sparse
Sides – jungle cock
Topping – golden pheasant tied long along top edge of wing

190   *Lough Neagh*

Lough Erne Mayfly size 8 to 10 wet lough fly.

Body – medium olive seal's fur

Rib – oval gold

Body and shoulder hackle – scarlet cock hackle

Shoulder hackle – grey speckled mallard dyed yellow

Tail – three cock pheasant tail fibres

Lough Melvin Mayfly (Sean Maguire) size 10 to 12 lough wet fly.

Body – white tape

Rib – silver wire

Body hackle – badger

Head hackle – dark sooty hackle topped with dark olive French partridge

Tail – pheasant tail fibres

Melvin Octopus (Sean Maguire) size 10/12 lough fly.

Body – golden olive seal's fur

Rib – silver wire

Hackle – Medium olive palmered

Head hackle – grey partridge dyed yellow

Tail – four strands glo bright green

Mosely Mayfly size 8 to 10 dry mayfly lough pattern.

Body – half and half mix of hare's ear and yellow seal's fur

Rib – fine oval gold tinsel

Hackle – medium olive and grizzle hackles with yellow cock hackle wound through them tied fan shaped on top of the fly and secured underneath with a few pheasant tail fibres

Tail – pheasant tail fibres

Murrough (Claret) size 8 to 10 wet lough sedge fly.

Body – dark claret seal's fur

Rib – fine oval gold tinsel

Hackle – red brown cock hackle palmered

Front hackle – red brown cock hackle

Wing – dark brown speckled hen

Mayflies

O'Conner's Green or Yellow May size 8 to 10 dry lough fly.

Body – natural raffia

Rib – red floss

Hackles – two good quality red game

Wings – duck flank dyed green or yellow and tied as split wings

Tail – three cock pheasant tail fibres

Silver Dabbler (Stuart McTeare) size 8 to 10 long shank wet lough fly.

Body – claret seal's fur well picked out

Rib – flat silver tinsel with extra silver wire if necessary to hold the hackle

Hackle – two ginger cock hackles palmered at the shoulder

Wing – bronze mallard tied long

Head – black silk built up

Tail – bronze mallard

Silver Spider size 12 to16 river wet fly.

Body – flat silver tinsel

Rib – fine silver wire

Hackle – sparse black hen

191

Westmeath (old traditional river/lough fly described by O'Gorman 1845) size 6 to 10 wet fly.
Body – yellow or olive seal's fur
Hackle – deep red
Wing – brown mallard
Tail – gold floss
Tag – bronze mallard
Eyes – red or black beads
Horns – spotted mallard

Yellow Gosling (lough Melvin fly) size 8 to 12 wet fly.
Body – golden olive seals fur
Rib – fine oval gold
Shoulder hackle – orange with grey speckled mallard dyed light olive in front
Tail – three cock pheasant tail fibres

Yellow Wulff size 8 to 10 dry lough fly popular for mayfly.
Body – yellow Antron or floss
Rib – glo brite floss no10
Hackle – two medium yellow cock hackles
Wing – brown bucktail or squirrel
Tail – brown bucktail or squirrel

FINALE

So there you have it, lake and river trout flies and tactics past and present from across the UK and Ireland, how they started, how they were developed and what they have become in the twenty-first century. During the long hours of research, contemplation and dissection of Scottish, English, Irish and Welsh many and varied trout fishing methods it has become abundantly clear that most of the techniques have been devised often over a long period of time to suit the region and its inherent conditions. Yes there has been some fashion following but by and large over time practical matters have held sway. Trout fishing never has been and never will be able to fall into the category of one size fits all. There is perhaps no such thing as clinical textbook fishing for the flies and techniques we use today for trout have to fit in with the locale, the nature of its waters, the main hatches, in short we must fish according to the nature of the beast. Trout are trout wherever you find them but I hope I have let you see better some of the subtle differences in your fishing for them.

If you learn only one lesson from this book let it be that you need to take time to watch, listen and learn from what the locals do and, if the wind and weather are right, you will almost immediately double your chances of success. Try to fish in harmony with your surroundings safe in the knowledge that you follow in the footsteps of many great anglers who have spent many years working out what works best on their local waters. We owe them a huge debt of gratitude. Let's help keep those great trout traditions as vibrant as they were when first devised...

The Author (photo by P. Trotter)

Appendix

Permission to Fish

Scotland

In Scotland there is no rod licence system and therefore all you need to obtain and usually pay for is permission to fish. Laws governing trout fishing and permits are slightly different relating to rivers and lochs. On rivers containing migratory fish like salmon and sea trout (and most of Scotland's rivers contain these species or have done so in the past) anglers are governed by the Salmon Act 1986 which details that it is an offence to fish for salmon even if you only want to catch trout, without obtaining a written permit (i.e. permission to fish) and you can be prosecuted. On lochs the situation is slightly different. In inland freshwaters where there are no migratory fish present the angler is governed by civil laws which are inordinately vague and in desperate need of an update. Basically no one even if he is lawfully on the bank of a loch has the right to fish it. Fishing rights belong solely to the landowner whose land fronts the loch. Permission to fish the loch is therefore given by the landowner or his appointees for example angling clubs or other lessees. However a good number of Scotland's lochs are now governed by Protection Orders and under these it is an offence in criminal law to fish without a permit. Since most of Scotland's trout fishing is very reasonably priced and permits normally available locally there is usually no problem. The brown trout season legally runs from 15 March to 6 October though note some waters make this a bit shorter say 1 April to 30 September. There is no close season for rainbows though some fisheries close for maintenance.

England and Wales

Permission to fish for trout in England and Wales is a bit different from Scotland. Before starting fishing in any watercourse you must obtain both an Environmental Agency rod licence and a written permit. Rod licences are widely available from post offices, retail outlets, sometimes at the fishing venues themselves and over the internet. This licence can be bought on a daily, weekly, monthly or yearly basis and you will often be asked by bailiffs to produce this document while fishing. In addition you will need a permit either in the form of a day, week or season ticket. Basically this means your angling is a bit more controlled than in the vast spaces of Scotland but as long as you do the appropriate paperwork before starting to fish you should not have any problem. Brown trout season runs 15 March to 6 October but there are slight variations here and there notably when there are sea trout amongst the browns. The rainbow trout season is longer with some fisheries only closing for a short period to allow maintenance or holidays.

Ireland

In Northern Ireland you will need to obtain a rod licence if you are fishing for salmon, sea trout or brown trout. In Southern Ireland you do not need a licence to fish for trout. Local permits to fish by the day, week or season are required on most waters for brown trout and migratory species in both Northern and Southern Ireland. The brown trout season in Ireland starts earlier than most in the UK and can run from 15 February to 12 October though 1 March to 30 September are the most common times. Rainbow trout fisheries are in the minority here and any close seasons for these vary – seek local advice.

SELECT BIBLIOGRAPHY

J Bailey, *Where to Fly Fish in Britain and Ireland*, New Holland
R C Bridgett, *Loch Fishing Theory and Practice*, Herbert Jenkins
G Bucknall, *The Bright Stream of Memory*, Swan Hill Press
J Gale, D Moore, P Gathercole, *Trout*, Boydell Press
W Earl Hodgson, *Trout Fishing*, A & C Black
Edmonds & Lee, *Brook & River Trouting*, Partridge Press
E Evans, *Traditional Fishing in Wales*, Carreg Gwalch
R Fogg, *A Handbook of North Country Flies*, Old Vicarage Publications
Frost and Brown, *The Trout*, Collins
W M Gallichan, *Fishing in Wales*, Robinson & Co
G Harris and M Morgan, *Successful Sea Trout Angling*, Blandford Press
H P Henzell, *Fishing for Sea Trout*, A & C Black
A Herd, *The Fly*, Medlar Press
J Waller Hills, *A History of Fly Fishing for Trout*, B Shurlock
T C Kingsmill Moore, *A Man May Fish*, Colin Smythe
Oliver Kite, *Nymph Fishing in Practice*, Swan Hill
A A Luce, *Fishing and Thinking*, Swan Hill
Maitland and Campbell, *Freshwater Fishes*, HarperCollins
Marquess of Granby and others, *The Trout – Fur Feather and Fin series*, Longmans
Daniel McCrea, *Fisherman's Forum*, Witherby Ltd
C B McCully, *A Dictionary of Fly Fishing*, Oxford University Press
Moc Morgan, *Trout and Salmon Flies of Wales*, Merlin Unwin
J C Mottram, *Trout Fisheries their Care and Preservation*, Herbert Jenkins Ltd
James O'Gorman, *Practice of Angling particularly as regards Ireland*, Fly Fishers Classic
    Library reprint
P O'Reilly, *Fly Fishing in Ireland*, Stackpole Books
E Phillips, *Trout in Lakes and Reservoirs*, Longmans
Plunket Greene, *Where the Bright Waters Meet*, Flyfishers Classic Library
J Roberts, *New Illustrated Dictionary of Trout Flies*, Unwin
Professor N W Simmonds, *Early Scottish Angling Literature*, Swan Hill Press
G E M Skues, *The Way of a Trout with a Fly*, A & C Black
W C Stewart, *The Practical Angler*, A & C Black
Stolz and Schnell (editors), *The Wildlife series – Trout*, Stackpole Books
J Todd, *Game Angling in the North of Ireland*, Blackstaff Guides
Rupert Watson, *The Trout – A Fisherman's Natural History*, Swan Hill Press

INDEX